HARD PRESS .NET

ISBN: 978129000909

Published by:
HardPress Publishing
8345 NW 66TH ST #2561
MIAMI FL 33166-2626

Email: info@hardpress.net
Web: http://www.hardpress.net

UNIVERSITY
OF CALIFORNIA
LOS ANGELES

SCHOOL OF LAW
LIBRARY

FEDERAL EMPLOYERS' LIABILITY ACT

Practitioner's Manual

DIGEST OF DECISIONS UNDER ACT

—

JUDICIAL LAW IN LANGUAGE OF COURT
INTERPRETATIONS

—

FORMS OF PLEADING UNDER REQUIREMENTS
of ACT

—

SAFETY APPLIANCE AND HOURS OF SERVICE ACTS

By

John A. Walgren

OF THE CHICAGO BAR

Associate Editor of Illinois Annotated Statutes and Continental Legal
History Series

—

CHICAGO
T. H. FLOOD & CO., PUBLISHERS
1916

TABLE OF CONTENTS

TABLE OF CONTENTS

TABLE OF CONTENTS

TABLE OF CONTENTS

FEDERAL EMPLOYERS' LIABILITY ACT.

"An Act relating to the Liability of Common Carriers by Railroad to Their Employees in Certain Cases.

Act April 22, 1908; *c.* 149; *as amended by Act April* 5, 1910; *c.* 145. 35 *Stat.* 65 *et seq.*
Compiled Statutes of the United States; Vol. 4, §§ 8657, *et seq.*

(Act 1908, c. 149, § 1) **Common carriers by railroad engaging in interstate or foreign commerce, liable for injuries to employees, from negligence.**

Every common carrier by railroad, while engaging in commerce between any of the several States or Territories, or between any of the States and Territories, or between the District of Columbia and any of the States or Territories, or between the District of Columbia or any of the States or Territories and any foreign nation or nations, shall be liable in damages to any person suffering injury while he is employed by such carrier in such commerce, or, in case of the death of such employee, to his or her personal representative, for the benefit of the surviving widow or husband and children of such employee; and, if none, then of such employee's parents; and, if none, then of the next of kin dependent upon such employee, for such injury or death resulting in whole or in part from the negligence of any of the officers, agents or employees of such carrier, or by reason of any defect or insufficiency, due to its negligence, in its cars, engines, appliances, machinery, track, roadbed, docks, boats, wharves, or other equipment. (35 Stat. 65.)

(Act 1908, c. 149, § 2.) **Common carriers in Territories, possessions, etc., likewise liable.**

Every common carrier by railroad in the Territories, the District of Columbia, the Panama Canal Zone, or other possessions of the United States shall be liable in damages to any person suffering injury while he is employed by such carrier in any of said jurisdictions, or, in case of the death of such employee, to his or her personal representative, for the benefit of the surviving widow or husband and children of such employee; and, if none, then of such employee's parents; and, if none, then of the next of kin dependent upon such employee, for such injury or death resulting in whole or in part from the negligence of any of the officers, agents, or employees of such carrier, or by reason of any defect or insufficiency, due to its negligence, in its cars, engines, appliances, machinery, track, roadbed, docks, boats, wharves, or other equipment (35 Stat. 65.)

(Act 1908, c. 149, § 3) **Contributory negligence not to bar recovery, but diminish damages, except where statute violated by carrier.**

In all actions hereafter brought against any such common carrier by railroad under or by virtue of any of the provisions of this Act to recover damages for personal injuries to an employee, or where such injuries have resulted in his death, the fact that the employee may have been guilty of contributory negligence shall not bar a recovery, but the damages shall be diminished by the jury in proportion to the amount of negligence attributable to such employee: Provided, That no such employee who may be injured or killed shall be held to have been guilty of contributory negligence in any case where the violation by such common carrier of any statute enacted for the safety of employees contributed to the injury or death of such employee. (35 Stat. 66.)

(Act 1908, c. 149, § 4.) **Assumption of risks of employment, no defense where violation of statute contributed to injury.**

In any action brought against any common carrier under or by virtue of any of the provisions of this Act to recover damages for injuries to, or the death of, any of its employees, such employee shall not be held to have assumed the risks of his employment in any case where the violation by such common carrier of any statute created for the safety of employees contributed to the injury or death of such employee. (35 Stat. 66.)

(Act 1908, c. 149, § 5.) **Contracts of exemption from liability to such extent void; Set-offs.**

Any contract, rule, regulation or device whatsoever, the purpose or intent of which shall be to enable any common carrier to exempt itself from any liability created by this Act, shall to that extent be void: Provided, That in any action brought against any such common carrier under or by virtue of any of the provisions of this Act, such common carrier may set off therein any sum it has contributed or paid to any insurance, relief benefit, or indemnity that may have been paid to the injured employee or the person entitled thereto on account of the injury or death for which said action was brought. (35 Stat. 66.)

Act April 22, 1908; *c.* 149, § 6; *as amended Act April* 5, 1910, c. 143, § 1. **Action to be commenced in two years. Jurisdiction of Federal and State Courts concurrent; no removal.**

No action shall be maintained under this Act unless commenced within two years from the day the cause of action accrued.

Under this Act an action may be brought in a (circuit court) of the United States in the district of the residence of the defendant, or in which the cause of action arose, or in which the defendant shall be doing business at the time of commencing such action. The jurisdiction of the courts of the United States under this Act shall be concurrent with that of the courts of the several States, and no case arising under this Act and brought in any state court of competent jurisdiction shall be removed to any court of the United States. (35 Stat. 66. 36 Stat. 291.)

(Amendment added second paragraph.)

(Circuit Court jurisdiction transferred to District Courts by Jud. Code §§ 289-291.)

(Act 1908, c. 149, § 7.) **Term "common carrier" to include receivers.**

The term "common carrier" as used in this Act shall include the receiver or receivers or other persons or corporations charged with the duty of the management and operation of the business of a common carrier. (35 Stat. 66.)

(Act 1908, c. 149, § 8) **Duty or liability under other Acts not impaired.**

Nothing in this Act shall be held to limit the duty or liability of common carriers or to impair the rights of their employees under any other Act or Acts of Congress or to affect the prosecution of any pending proceeding or right of action under the Act of Congress entitled "An Act relating to liability of common carriers in the District of Columbia and Territories and to common carriers engaged in commerce between the States and between the States and foreign nations to their employees," approved June eleventh, nineteen hundred and six. (35 Stat. 66.)

Act of April 22, 1908. c. 149 § 9, *as amended Act April* 5, 1910. *c.* 143, § 2) **Survival of right of action of injured employee.**

Any right of action given by this Act to a person suffering injury shall survive to his or her personal representative, for the benefit of the surviving widow or husband and children of such employee, and, if none, then of such employee's parents; and, if none, then of the next of kin dependent upon such employee, but in such cases there shall be only one recovery for the same injury. (36 Stat. 291.) (This section was added as § 9 of the Act of 1908 by amending Act of 1910, c. 143, § 2.)

Constitution—Act is in accord with—

Employers' Liability Act of Congress of April 22, 1908, and Amendment of April 5, 1910, are in harmony with and not repugnant to the Constitution of the United States:—

> *Mondou* v *New York, N. H. & H. R. R.;* 223 U. S. 1; 32 Sup. Ct. Rep. 169; 56 L. Ed. 327; 38 L. R. A. (N. S.) 44; rev: 82 Conn. 373; 73 Atl. Rep. 762.
>
> *Illinois Central R. R.* v *Behrens,* 233 U. S. 473; 34 Sup. Ct. 648; 58 L. Ed. 105.
>
> *Michigan Central RR.* v *Vreeland,* 227 U. S. 59; 33 Sup. Ct. 192; 57 L. Ed. 192; rev: 189 Fed. 495.
>
> *Philadelphia &c RR.* v *Schubert,* 224 U. S. 603; 32 Sup. Ct. 589; 56 L. Ed. 9.
>
> *Chicago &c RR.* v *McGuire,* 229 U. S. 549; 33 Sup. Ct. 259; 55 L. Ed. 238.
>
> *First Employers' Liability Cases,* 207 U. S. 463; 28 Sup. Ct. 143; 52 L. Ed. 297.
>
> *Second Employers' Liability Cases,* 223 U. S. 603.
>
> *El Paso &c Ry.* v *Gutierrez,* 215 U. S. 87.
>
> *Kelly's Admx.* v *Chesapeake &c RR.,* 201 Fed. Rep. 602.
>
> *Cain* v *Southern Pac. Ry.,* 199 Fed. 211.
>
> *Walsh* v *New York &c RR.,* 173 Fed. 494.
>
> *St. Louis &c RR.* v *Conly,* 187 Fed. 949.
>
> *Zikos* v *Oregon &c Co.,* 179 Fed. 893.
>
> *Owens* v *Chicago &c Ry.,* 79 Fed. 893.

The Supreme Court of the United States, in upholding the Act, said:

"The departures from the common law made by the portions of the Act against which objection is leveled are these: (a) The rule that the negligence of one employe resulting in injury to another was not to be attributed to their common employer is displaced by a rule imposing upon the employer responsibility for such injury, as was done at common law when the injured person was not an employe; (b) the rule exonerating an employer from liability for injury sustained by an employe through the concurring negligence of the employer and employe is abrogated in all instances where the employer's violation of a statute enacted for the safety of his employes contributes to the injury, and in other instances is displaced by the rule of comparative negligence, whereby the exoneration is only from a proportional part of the damages corresponding to the amount of negligence attributable to the employe; (c) the rule that an employe was deemed to assume the risk of injury, even if due to the employer's negligence, where the employe voluntarily entered or remained in the service with an actual or presumed knowledge of the conditions out of which the risk arose, is abrogated in all instances where the employer's violation of a statute enacted for the safety of his employes contributed to the injury; and (d) the rule denying a right of action for the death of one person caused by the wrongful act or neglect of another is displaced by a rule vesting such right of action in the personal representatives of the deceased for the benefit of designated relatives.   *   *   *   *

"A person has no property, no vested interest, in any rule of the common law.   *   *   *   *

"The natural tendency of the changes described is to impel the carriers to avoid or prevent the negligent acts or omissions which are made the basis of the rights of recovery which the statute creates and defines; and, as whatever makes for that end tends to promote the safety of employes and to advance the commerce in which they are engaged, we entertain no doubt that in making those changes Congress acted within the limits of the discretion confided to it by the Constitution. We are not unmindful that the end was being measurably attained through the remedial legislation of the several States, but that legislation has been far from uniform, and it undoubtedly rested with Congress to determine whether a national law operating uniformly in all the States upon all carriers by railroad engaged in interstate commerce, would better subserve the needs of that commerce.

"Nor is it a valid objection that the act embraces instances when the causal negligence is that of an employe engaged in intra-state commerce; for such negligence, when operating injuriously upon an employe engaged in interstate commerce, has the same effect upon that commerce as if the negligent employe was also engaged therein.

"Next in order is the objection that the provision in Sec. 5, declaring void any contract, rule, regulation or device, the purpose or intent of which is to enable the carrier to exempt itself from the liability which the Act creates, is repugnant to the Fifth Amendment of the Constitution as an unwarranted interference with the liberty of contract. * * * * If Congress possesses the power to impose that liability, which we here hold that it does, it also possesses the power to insure its efficacy by prohibiting any contract, rule, regulation or device in evasion of it.

"The duties of common carriers in respect of the safety of their employes, while both are engaged in commerce among the States, and the liability of the former for injuries sustained by the latter, while both are so engaged, have a real or substantial relation to such commerce, and therefore are within the range of this power. * * * Congress may legislate about the agents and instruments of interstate commerce, and about the conditions under which those agencies and instruments perform the work of interstate commerce, whenever such legislation bears, or in the exercise of a fair legislative discretion can be deemed to bear upon the reliability or promptness or economy or security or utility of the interstate commerce act."

Second Liability Cases, 223 U. S. 1.

Congress has power to regulate liability of carrier, whether the particular service being performed at the time of injury, isolatedly considered, is in interstate or intra-state commerce.

Illinois C. R. R. v *Behrens*, 233 U. S. 473.

Act makes no unjust discrimination in precluding removal of causes.

Kelly's Admx. v *Chesapeake &c Ry.*, 201 F. 602.

Act of June 11, 1906, was declared invalid because its provisions regarding interstate commerce were so intermingled with intra-state matters as to render entire Act void.

"Concluding, as we do, that the Statute (Act of June 11, 1906), whilst it embraces subjects within the authority of Congress to regulate commerce, also includes subjects not within its constitutional power, and that the two are so interblended in the statute that they are incapable of separation, we are of the opinion that the courts below rightly held the Statute to be repugnant to the Constitution and non-enforcible."

First Employer's Liability Cases, 207 U. S. 463.

Chicago &c Ry. v *Hackett*, 228 U. S. 559.

Hozie v *New York &c RR.*, 82 Conn. 352; 73 Atl. 754.

Howard v *Illinois Central RR.*, 207 U. S. 463; 28 S. C. 141; 52 L. Ed. 297.

Act of 1906 held repugnant to Constitution of Oklahoma and locally inapplicable.

Chicago &c Ry. v *Holliday*, Okla., 145 Pac. 786.

"In the aspect of the Act of 1906, Congress proceeded within its constitutional power, and with the intention to regulate the matter in the District of Columbia and Territories, irrespective of the interstate commerce feature of the act."

El Paso &c Ry. v *Gutierreg, Admr.*, 215 U. S. 87; Aff. 117 S. W. 426.

State Law—Act supersedes—

Act, wherever applicable, supersedes constitutions, statutes and common law of the States, and affords the exclusive remedy:

Taylor v *Taylor,* 232 U. S. 363; 34 L. Ed. 350; rev: 204 N. Y. 135; 97 N. E. Rep. 502; which affd: 144 App. Div. 634; 129 N. Y. S. 378.

Seaboard Air Line Ry. v *Horton,* 233 U. S. 492; 34 S. C. 635; 58 L. Ed. 1062.

Gulf &c Ry. v *McGinnis,* 228 U. S. 173; 33 S. C. 426; 57 L. Ed. 785.

Michigan Central Ry. v *Vreeland,* 227 U. S. 59; 33 S. C. 192; 57 L. Ed. 417; Ann. Cas. 1914 C. 176.

American RR. v *Didricksen,* 227 U. S. 145; 33 S. C. 224; 57 L.Ed. 456.

Missouri &c Ry. v *Wulf,* 226 U. S. 570; 33 S. C. 135; 57 L. Ed. 355; Ann. Cas. 1914 B. 134.

Second Employers' Liability Cases, 223 U. S. 1; 32 S. C. 169; 56 L .Ed. 327; 38 L. R. A. (N. S.) 44.

Toledo &c Ry. v *Slavin,* 236 U. S. 454; 35 S. C. 306; Rev: 88 Oh. St. 536.

Kansas City S. Ry. v *Leslie,* 238 U. S. 599.

North Carolina RR. v. *Zachary,* 232 U. S. 248.

St. Louis &c Ry. v *Hesterly,* 228 U. S. 70; 33 S. C. 703; rev: 98 Ark. 240; 57 S. E. Rep. 1031.

St. Louis &c Ry. v *Seale,* 229 U. S. 156.

Pedersen v *Delaware &c Ry.* 229 U. S. 146.

Central Vermont Ry. v *White's Admx.,* 238 U. S. 507; Aff. 87 Vt. 330.

Grand Trunk Ry. v *Lindsay,* 233 U. S. 42.

Wabash Ry. v *Hayes,* 234 U. S. 86.

Delaware &c Ry. v *Troxell,* 200 Fed. 44; 118 C. C. A. 272.

Delaware etc. Ry. v *Yurkonis,* 220 Fed. 429; Aff. 213 Fed. 537; Appeal dismissed 238 U. S. 439.

Taylor v *Southern Ry.,* 178 Fed. 380.

Cound v *Atchison &c Ry.,* 173 Fed. 527.

Clark v *Southern Ry.,* 175 Fed. 122.

DeAtley v *Chesapeake &c Ry.,* 201 Fed. 602.

Kamboris v *Oregon &c Ry.,* .. Or. ..; 146 Pac. 1097.

South Covington &c Ry. v *Finan's Admx.,* 153 Ky. 340; 155 S. W. 742.

Midland Valley RR. v *Ennis,* .. Ark. ..; 159 S. W. 214.

Wagner v *Chicago &c Ry.,* 265 Ill. 245; 106 N. E. 809; Aff. 180 Ill. App. 196; Reh. den. 107 N. E. 673.

Vandalia RR. v *Stringer,* .. Ind. ..; 106 N. E. 865.

Ex Parte Coast Line Ry., .. Ala. (1914) 67 So. Rep. 256.

Gee v *Lehigh Valley RR.,* 163 App. Div. 274; 148 N. Y. S. 882.

Southern Ry. v *Howerton,* Ind. 1914, 105 N. E. 1025; Reh. den. 106 N. E. 369.

Erie RR. v *Welsh,* Ohio 1913, 105 N. E. 189.

Miller v *Kansas City Ry.,* 180 Mo. App. 371; 168 S. W. 336.

Hogarty v *Phila. &c RR.,* 245 Pa. St. 443; 91 App. 854.

Oberlin v *Oregon &c Nav. Co.,* 142 Pac. 554.

Penny v *New Orleans &c RR.,* 135 La. 962; 66 So. Rep. 313.

Michigan Central RR. v. *Michigan RR. Com.,* 148 N. W. 800.

Robinson v *Louisville &c Ry.*, 160 Ky. 235; 169 S. W. 831.

Armbruster v *Chicago R. I. & P. Ry.*, 147 N. Y. 337.

Devine v *Chicago, R. I. & P. Ry.*, 185 Ill. App. 488; Affd. 107 N. E. 595.

Lauer v *Northern Pac. Ry.*, 145 Pac. 606.

Louisville &c Ry. v. *Kemp.*, 140 Ga. 657; 79 S. E. 558.

McGarvey's Guardian v *McGarvey's Admr.*, 163 Ky. 242; 173 S. W. Rep. 765.

Corbett v *Boston &c Ry.*, 219 Mass. 351; 107 N. E. 60.

Thompson v *Wabash RR.*, Mo. 1914, 171 S. W. 364.

Melzner v *Northern Pac. Ry.*, 46 Mont. 277; 127 Pac. 1002.

Rich v *St. Louis &c Ry.*, 166 Mo. App. 379; 148 S. W. 1011.

Eastern Ry. of New Mexico v *Ellis*, Texas 1913, 153 S. W. 701.

Copper River &c Ry. v *Henney*, 211 Fed. 459.

Cole v *Atchison &c Ry.*, 92 Kan. 132; 139 Pac. 1157.

Fulgham v *Midland Ry.*, 167 Fed. 660.

The Passaic, 190 Fed. 644.

Southern Pac. Ry. v *McGinnis*, 174 Fed. 649.

Missouri &c Ry. v *Lenahan*, 135 Pac. 383.

Kambroris v *Oregon &c Co.*, 146 Pac. 1097.

Cincinnati &c Ry. v *Bonham*, 130 Tenn. 435; 171 S. W. 79.

Rivera v *Atchison &c Ry.*, 149 S. W. Rep. 223.

Burtnett v. *Erie Ry.*, 144 N. Y. S. 969; 159 App. Div. 712.

White v. *Central Vt. RR.*, 89 Atl. 618.

Niles v. *Central Vt. RR.*, 89 Atl. 629.

Southern Ry. v *Jacobs,* 81 S. E. Rep. 99.
Vaughan v *St. Louis &c Ry.,* 177 Mo. App. 155;
164 S. W. 144.

"By this Act Congress has undertaken to cover the subject of the liability of railroad companies to their employes while engaged in interstate commerce. This exertion of power which is granted in express terms must supersede all legislation over the same subject by the States. * * * It therefore follows that in respect of state legislation prescribing the liability of such carriers for injuries to their employes while engaged in interstate commerce this Act is paramount and exclusive, and must remain so until Congress shall again remit the subject to the reserved police power of the States."

Mich. Cent. RR. Co. v *Vreeland,* 227 U. S. 59.

"It is settled that since Congress, by the Act of 1908, took possession of the field of the employers' liability to employes in interstate transportation by rail, all state laws upon the subject are superseded."

Seaboard Air Line v *Horton,* 233 U. S. 492; rev: 162 N. C. 77.

Citing Second Employers' Liability Cases, 223 U. S. 155.

"In order to bring the case within the terms of the Federal Act defendant must have been at the time of the occurrence in question, engaged as a common carrier in interstate commerce, and plaintiff's intestate must have been employed by said carrier in such commerce. If these facts appeared, the Federal Act governed, to the exclusion of the statutes of the state."

North Carolina RR. v. *Zachary,* 232 U. S. 248; rev. 156 N. C. 496.

The Act governs and must be enforced even where employe and railroad fail to plead it.

"If, without amendment, the case proceeded with the proof showing that the right of the plaintiff and the liability of the defendant had to be measured by the Federal statute, it was not error to apply and enforce the provisions of that law."

> *Toledo &c RR.* v *Slavin*, 236 U. S. 454; rev. 88 Oh. St. 536.
>
> *St. Louis &c Ry.* v *Seale*, 229 U. S. 156.

Even though intra-state operations be involved.

> *Flanders* v *Georgia S. &c Ry.*, 67 So. 68.

Is supreme law of the land and excludes conflicting state law.

> *Toledo &c Ry.* v *Slavin*, 236 U. S. 454.

Excludes state and common law.

> *Easter* v *Virginia Ry.*, 86 S. E. 37.
>
> *Shannon* v *Boston &c RR.*, 77 N. H. 349; 92 Atl. 167.
>
> *Hawkins* v *St. Louis &c Ry.*, 174 S. W. Rep. 129.
>
> *Erie RR.* v *Welsh*, 105 N. E. Rep. 189.
>
> *Hogarty* v *Philadelphia Ry.*, 245 Atl. 443.

Excludes conflicting constitutions and statutes.

> *St. Louis &c Ry.* v *Snowden*, 149 Pac. 1083.

Exclusive where applicable.

> *Vickery* v *New London &c Ry.*, 87 Conn. 634; 89 Atl. 277.

Controls when complaint states a case under Act and also under state law, and former is alone applicable.

> *Peck* v *Boston &c Ry.*. 223 Fed. 448.

Precludes action under state law.

> *Dewberry* v *Southern Ry.*. 175 Fed. 307.

Act must be enforced by state court although not in harmony with local law.

> *Gee* v *Lehigh Valley RR.*, 148 N. Y. S. 882; 163 App. Div. 274.

Act covers every act of negligence for which railroad might be liable to employe engaged in interstate commerce.

> *DeAtley* v *Chesapeake &c RR.*, 201 Fed. 591.

If a liability does not exist under Act, it does not exist by virtue of any state legislation on the same subject.

> *Michigan Central RR.* v *Vreeland*, 227 U. S. 59.
> *Miller* v *Kansas City &c Ry.*, 180 Mo. App. 371;
> 168 S. W. 336.

Provision in a State constitution against defense of assumed risk is overcome.

> *Bramlett* v *Southern Ry.*, 98 S. C. 319; 82 S. E.
> 501.

Act controls although its provisions have not been pleaded or pressed.

> *Grand Trunk Ry.* v *Lindsay*, 233 U. S. 42; 34 S.
> C. 581; 201 Fed. 836; 120 C. C. A. 166.

Is only basis of recovery.

> *Louisville &c Ry.* v *Strange's Admx.*, 156 Ky.
> 439; 161 S. W. 239.

A state law interfering is not invalid but inoperative while Act is in force.

> *Houston &c Ry.* v *Bright*, 228 U. S. 559.
> *Chicago &c Ry.* v *Hackett*, 156 S. W. Rep. 304.

Workmen's compensation acts are not applicable to cases of employes injured while engaged in interstate commerce traffic, and no recovery may be had under them.

> *Staley* v *Illinois Central Ry.*, Ill. 109 N. E. 342; Rev. 186 Ill. App. 593.
>
> *Smith* v *Industrial Accident Com.*, 147 Pac. 600.
>
> *Rannsville* v *Central RR.*, N. J. 94 Atl. Rep. 392.
>
> *Winfeld* v *New York Central Ry.*, 153 N. Y. S. 499.
>
> *Southern Pac. Ry.* v *Pissberg*, Col. 151 Pac. Rep. 277.

Act precludes recovery under Workmen's Compensation Act by employe whose injury was not caused by master's negligence, where the facts bring the case within interstate commerce.

> *Smith* v *Industrial Accident Commission of California*, 147 Pac. 600.

Interstate Commerce—Employer must be engaged in—

"In order to bring the case within the terms of the Federal Act, defendant must have been at the time of the occurrence in question engaged as a common carrier in interstate commerce, 'and plaintiff's intestate must have been employed by said carrier in such commerce. If these facts appear, the Federal act governs, to the exclusion of the statutes of the state."

> *North Carolina R. R. Co.* v *Zachary*, 232 U. S. 248.
>
> *Second Employers' Liability Cases*, 223 U. S. 1.
>
> *St. Louis & San Francisco Ry* v *Seale*, 229 U. S. 156.
>
> *Pederson* v *Delaware &c Ry.* 229 U. S. 146; 33 S. Ct. 648; 57 L. Ed. 1125; Ann. Cas. 1914, C. 153.
>
> *Illinois Central Ry.* v *Behrens*, 233 U. S. 473; 34 S. Ct. 646; 58 L. Ed. 1051; Ann. Cas. 1914, C. 163.
>
> *Erie RR.* v *Jacobus*, 211 Fed. 335.
>
> *Zikos* v *Oregon &c Ry.* 179 Fed. 893.
>
> *Central Ry* v *Colasurdo*, 192 Fed. 901; 113 C. C. A. 379.
>
> *Montgomery* v *Southern Pac. Ry.*, 64 Or. 597; 131 Pac. 507; 47 L. R. A. (N. S.) 13.
>
> *Miller* v *Kansas City &c Ry.*, 180 Mo. App. 371; 168 S. W. 336.
>
> *Horton* v *Oregon &c Ry.*, 72 Wash. 503; 130 Pac. 897; 47 L. R. A. (N. S.) 8.
>
> *Illinois Central RR.* v *Rogers*, 221 Fed. 52.
>
> *Darr* v *Baltimore &c Ry.*, 197 Fed. 665.
>
> *Gordon* v *New Orleans &c Ry.*, 64 So. Rep. 1014.
>
> *St. Louis &c Ry.* v *Hesterly*, 135 S. W. Rep. 874.
>
> *Charleston &c Ry.* v *Anchors*, 73 S. E. Rep. 551.
>
> *Atchison* v *Pitts*, 145 Pac. Rep. 1148.
>
> *Neil* v *Idaho &c Ry.*, 22 Idaho 74; 125 Pac. 331.

"The term 'commerce' comprehends more than the mere exchange of goods. It embraces commercial intercourse in all its branches, including transportation of passengers and property by common carriers, whether carried on by water or land."

> *Second Employers' Liability Cases*, 223 U. S. 1, 46.

Interstate Commerce—Employee must be engaged in—

"Giving to the words 'suffering injury while he is employed by such carrier in such commerce' their natural meaning, as we think must be done, it is clear that Congress intended to confine its action to injuries occurring when the particular service in which the employe is engaged is a part of interstate commerce. The true test always is: Is the work in question a part of the interstate commerce in which the carrier is engaged? The true test is the nature of the work being done at the time of injury."

Illinois Central RR. v *Behrens,* 233 U. S. 473.

Mondou v *New York &c R. R.,* 223 U. S. 1.

Seaboard &c Ry. v *Moon,* 228 U. S. 433.

St. Louis &c Ry. v *Seale,* 229 U. S. 156.

North Carolina R. R. v *Zachary,* 232 U.. S. 248;

Grand Trunk &c Ry. v *Lindsay,* 223 U. S. 42.

"The scope of the statute is so broad that it covers a vast field about which there can be no discussion. But owing to the fact that, during the same day, railroad employes often and rapidly pass from one class of employment to another, the courts are constantly called upon to decide those close questions where it is difficult to define the line which divides the state from interstate business. The matter is not to be decided by considering the physical position of the employe at the moment of injury. If he is hurt in the course of his employment while going to a car to perform an interstate duty, or if he is injured while preparing an engine for an interstate trip, he is entitled to the benefits of the Federal Act, although the accident occurred prior to the actual coupling of the engine to the interstate cars.

"This case is entirely different from that of *Illinois Central R. R.* v *Behrens*, 233 U. S. 473, for there the train of empty cars was running between two points in the same state. The fact that they might soon thereafter be used in interstate business did not affect their intra-state status at the time of the injury; for, if the fact that a car had been recently engaged in interstate commerce, or was expected soon to be used in such commerce, brought them within the class of interstate vehicles, the effect would be to give every car on the line that character. Each case must be decided in the light of the particular facts with a view of determining whether at the time of the injury, the employe is engaged in interstate business, or in an act which is so directly and immediately connected with such business as substantially to form a part or a necessary incident thereof."

New York Central &c R. R. v *Carr*, 238 U. S. 260; Aff. 158 App. Div. 891.

"It is argued that because the deceased fireman had not previously participated in any movements of interstate freight, and the through cars had not as yet been attached to his engine, his employment in interstate commerce was still in futuro. It seems to us, however, that his acts in inspecting, oiling, firing and preparing his engine for the trip were acts performed as a part of interstate commerce, and the circumstance that the interstate freight cars had not as yet been coupled is legally insignificant.

"Again it is said that because deceased had left his engine and was going to his boarding-house, he was engaged upon a personal errand, and not upon the carrier's business. Assuming that the evidence fairly tended to indicate the boarding-house as his destination, it nevertheless also appears that deceased was shortly to depart upon his run, having just prepared his engine for the purpose, and that he had not gone beyond the limits of the railroad yard when he was struck. There is nothing to indicate that his brief visit to the boarding-house was at all out of the ordinary, or was inconsistent with his duty to his employer. It seems to us clear that the man was still 'on duty' and employed in commerce, notwithstanding his temporary absence from the locomotive engine. We conclude that with the facts necessary to bring the case within the Federal Act, there was evidence that at least was sufficient to go to the jury."

North Carolina R. R. v Zachary, 232 U. S. 248;
Rev. 156 N. C. 496.

"The deceased was employed by defendant as a yard clerk, and his principal duties were those of examining incoming and outgoing trains and making a record of the numbers and initials of the cars, of inspecting and making a record of the seals on the car doors, of checking the cars with the conductors' lists and of putting cards or labels on the cars to guide switching crews in breaking up incoming and making up outgoing trains. His duties related both to intra-state and interstate traffic, and at the time of his injury he was on his way through the yard to one of the tracks therein to meet an incoming freight train from Oklahoma, composed of several cars, ten of which were loaded with freight. The purpose with which he was going to the train was that of taking the numbers of the cars and otherwise performing his duties in respect to them. While so engaged he was struck and fatally injured by a switch engine, which it is claimed was being negligently operated by other employes in the yard.

"The train from Oklahoma was not only an interstate train but was engaged in the movement of interstate freight, and the duty which the deceased was performing was connected with that movement, not indirectly or remotely, but directly and immediately. The interstate transportation was not ended merely because that yard was a terminal for that train, nor even if the cars were not going to points beyond. Whether they were going further or were to stop at that station, it still was necessary that the train be broken up and the cars taken to the appropriate tracks for making up outgoing trains or for unloading or delivering freight, and this was as much a part of interstate transportation as was the movement across the state line."

St. Louis &c Ry. v Seale, 229 U. S. 156.

"Tracks and bridges are as indispensable to interstate commerce by railroad as are engines and cars, and sound economic reasons unite with settled rules of law in demanding that all of these instrumentalities be kept in repair. The security, expedition and efficiency of the commerce depends in a large measure upon this being done. Indeed, the statute now before us proceeds upon the theory that the carrier is charged with the duty of exercising appropriate care to prevent or correct any defect or insufficiency * * * in its cars, engines, appliances, machinery, tracks, roadbed, works, boats, wharves, or other equipment used in interstate commerce. But independently of the statute we are of the opinion that the work of keeping such instrumentalities in a proper state of repair, while thus used, is so closely related to such commerce as to be in practice and in legal contemplation a part of it. The contention to the contrary proceeds upon the assumption that interstate commerce by railroad can be separated into its several elements and the nature of each determined regardless of its relation to others or to the business as a whole. But this is an erroneous assumption. The true test always is: 'Is the work in question a part of the interstate commerce in which the carrier is engaged?' See *McCall v California*, 136 U. S. 104; *Second Employers' Liability Cases; Zikos v Oregon R. N. Co.*, 179 Fed. 893; *Central Ry. v Colazurdo*, 192 Fed. 901; *Darr v Baltimore & O. Ry.*, 197 Fed. 665; *Northern Pac. Ry. v Maerkl*, 198 Fed. 1. Of course, we are not here concerned with the construction of tracks, bridges, engines or cars, which have not as yet become instrumentalities in such commerce, but only with the work of maintaining them in proper condition after they have become such instrumentalities and during their use as such. True, a track or bridge may be used in both interstate and intra-state commerce, but when it is so used, it is none the less an instrumentality of the former; nor does its double use prevent the employment of those who are engaged in its repair or in keeping it in suitable condition for use from being an employment in interstate commerce. The point is made that the plaintiff was not at the time of his injury engaged in removing the old girder and inserting the new one but was merely carrying to the place where that work was to be done, some of the materials to be used therein. We think there is no merit in this. It was necessary to the repair of the bridge that the materials be at hand, and the act of taking them there was a part of the work. In other words, it was a minor task which was essentially a part of the larger one, as is the case when an engineer takes his engine from the roundhouse to the track on which are the cars he is to haul in inter-intra-state commerce."

. . . ."*Pedersen v Delaware &c Ry.*, 229 U. S. 146.

"*Lamphere v Oregon R. & N. Co.*, 196 Fed. 338.

"*Horton v Oregon &c Co.*, 130 Pac. 897.

"*Johnson v Southern Pac. Co.*, 196 U. S. 1.

"In *Pedersen* v *Delaware &c Ry.*, 229 U. S. 146; 33 S. C. 648; 57 L. Ed. 1125, an employe of an interstate railway carrier was killed while carrying a sack of rivets to be used on the morrow in repairing a bidge over which regularly passed both kinds of commerce, and although he was killed by a train operating wholly within the state where the accident happened, yet it was held by the United States Supreme Court that the case came within the Federal Act, because the bridge to be repaired was habitually used in interstate commerce as well as the other kind.

"In *Horton* v *Oregon &c Co.*, 72 Wash. 503, 130 Pac. 897, 47 L. R. A. (N. S.) 8, the plaintiff decedent was in charge of a pumping station on the line of defendants' railroad at a point where both kinds of commerce passed over the track, and it was his duty to keep the tank filled from which locomotives took water while engaged in hauling all kinds of cars destined to points within and without the state where the accident occurred. He was killed by one of defendants' trains while returning from his work to his home. It was there decided that he was engaged in interstate commerce.

"In *Johnson* v *Great Northern Ry.*, 178 Fed. 643, 102 C. C. A. 89, the injured plaintiff in discharge of his duty was examining a defective coupling on an empty car which stood on the switch track waiting to be returned to another state. He was hurt by a switching engine in the yard having kicked a car against him. It was held that he was employed in interstate commerce.

"In *Northern Pac. Ry.* v *Maerkl.* 198 Fed. 1, 117 C. C. A. 237, a carpenter was injured while repairing a car used indiscriminately in both kinds of commerce, and it was held that the Act applied. In *Jones* v *Chesapeake &c Ry.*, 149 Ky. 566, 149 S. W. 951, the plaintiff was engaged in repairing a sidetrack of a railroad engaged in interstate commerce, and by the negligence of his fellow servants his thumb was mashed between the ends of rails which were being laid. It was held that the case came within the national legislation on the subject. The doctrine of the Mondou and Pedersen cases is that if the injury to the employe appreciably affects the conduct of interstate commerce by a railway carrier, it is within the purview of the Federal Act, and must be controlled by the statute, although the transaction in dispute may be closely connected with local traffic."

Oberlin v *Oregon &c N. Co.*, 71 Or. 177; 142 Pac. Rep. 554.

"The important inquiry is as to what the employe was doing at the time the accident occurred; and it appears without dispute in this record that the employe had finished the duties required of him by prior orders of the master and was, at the time of the injury, proceeding to the master's office for further orders and direction as to his service, so that he was not then and there employed in moving or handling cars engaged in interstate commerce. That service had been fully completed and ended, and he had not re-engaged in any similar employment, so there is no evidence in this record tending to prove that at the time the accident actually happened, this plaintiff was then and there engaged in interstate commerce, and the mere fact that shortly before that time he had been so engaged, or that the next service his master would require would be of interstate character, cannot and does not establish the fact that at the time of the injury he was so engaged."

Erie R. R. v *Welsh*, Ohio 1913, 105 N. E. Rep. 189.

The employe's relation must be so close and direct to interstate commerce that his injury tended to stop or delay movement of train engaged therein.

> *Shanks* v *Delaware &c Ry.,* 163 App. Div. 565;
> 148 N. Y. S. 1034.

The particular service must be part of interstate commerce.

> *Patry* v *Chicago &c Ry.,* 265 Ill. 310; 106 N. E.
> 843; Rev. 185 Ill. App. 361.
>
> *Baltimore &c Ry.* v *Darr,* 124 C. C. A. 565; 204
> Fed. 751; Aff. 197 Fed. 665.
>
> *Missouri &c Ry.* v *Fesmin,* 150 S. W. 201.

Act applies to every person whom Congress could include.

> *Horton* v *Oregon &c R. N. Co.,* 72 Wash. 503; 130
> Pac. 897.

Employe's being **in performance of his duty** must be shown.

> *Hobbs* v *Great Northern Ry.*, 80 Wash. 678; 142 Pac. 20.
>
> *Devine* v *Chicago &c Ry.*, 185 Ill. App. 488; Aff. 266 Ill. 248; 107 N. E. 595.
>
> *Bower* v *Chicago &c Ry.*, 96 Neb. 419; 148 N. W. 145.

Hostler's helper held not acting outside of duties.

> *Texas &c Ry.* v *Harvey*, 228 U. S. 319; 33 S. C. 518; Aff. 184 Fed. 990; 160 C. C. A. 668.

CONDUCTOR of freight train, who was injured while assisting in transferring, from one yard to another, cars then used in interstate commerce, is included in provisions of Act.

> *Wagner* v *Chicago & A. Ry.*, 180 Ill. App. 196.
> *See: Peery* v *Illinois Central R. R.*, 128 Minn. 119; 150 N. W. 382.

Although his run within state, included.

> *Pary* v *Illinois Central R. R.*, 143 N. W. 724.

Freight conductor, returning with only caboose, and hauling dead engine to a terminal, excluded.

> *McAuliffe* v *New York Central &c R. R.*, 150 N. Y. S. 512; 164 App. Div. 846.

Conductor getting train ready for inter- and intrastate freight, included.

> *Neil* v *Idaho &c R. R.*, 22 Idaho 74; 125 Pac. 331.

Extra conductor, riding to serve on work train, excluded.

> *Feaster* v *Phila. & R. Ry.*, 197 Fed. 580.

ENGINEER switching cars from train which he had just brought in from another state, included.

> *Kansas City &c Ry.* v *Pope,* 152 S. W. 185; Reh. den. 153 S. W. 163.
>
> See: *Hearst* v *St. Louis &c Ry.,* 173 S. W. 86.

BRAKEMAN carrying ice for interstate train, included.

> *Illinois Central R. R.* v *Nelson,* 203 Fed. 956.

Brakeman on interstate passenger train included.

> *Cincinnati &c Ry.* v *Goode,* 155 Ky. 153; 159 S. W. 695; Mod. on reh. 153 Ky. 247; 154 S. W. 941.
>
> *Oberlin* v *Oregon &c N. Co.,* 71 Or. 177; 142 Pac. 554.

Brakeman, injured by negligence of fellow-servant, working on intra-state car, included.

> *Carr* v *New York Central &c R. R.,* 136 N. Y. S. 501; 79 Mis. Rep. 346.

Brakeman, looking for tin cup for interstate train, included.

> *Baltimore &c R. R.* v *Whitacre,* 124 Md. 411; 92 Atl. 1060.

Brakeman on interstate train, assisting in switching and uncoupling cars to allow train to proceed, included.

> *New York Central Ry.* v *Carr,* 238 U. S. 260; Aff. 158 App. Div. 891.

Brakeman on pick-up train, containing interstate freight, setting brake on intra-state car, included.

> *New York &c R. R.* v *Carr,* 35 S. C. 780.

Brakeman, running an extra, lone engine, between intra-state points, excluded.

> *Wright* v *Chicago &c Ry.,* 143 N. W. 220.

FIREMAN, firing engine to be attached to interstate train, included.

> *Lonsellita* v *New York Central &c R. R.,* 94 Atl. 804.

Locomotive fireman on way to station to be transported to a distant point to fire interstate engine, excluded.

> *Lamphere* v *Oregon R. & N. Co.,* 193 Fed. 248; reversed in 196 Fed. 336.

SWITCHMAN of interstate, together with intrastate, trains, included.

> *Otos* v *Great Northern Ry.,* 128 Minn., 283; 150 N. W. 922.

Switching coal cars, containing interstate shipment, for dumping into bunkers, for use of interstate locomotives, included.

> *Barlow* v *Lehigh Valley R. R.,* 143 N. Y. S. 1053; 158 App. Div. 768.

Member of switching crew, moving oil from oil car for interstate train, included.

> *Montgomery* v *Southern Pac. Co.,* 131 Pac. 507.

Switching crew head, included. See:

> *Vandalia R. R.* v *Holland,* 108 N. E. 580.

Switchman—switching train of cars to be classified, inspected and assembled, excluded from safety appliance act.

> *United States* v *New York Central,* 205 Fed 428.

Switching in yards freight in transit, included.

> *Rich* v *St. Louis &c Ry.,* 166 Mo. App. 379; 148 S. W. 1011.

Switchman, handling inter- and intra-state cars just prior to death, included.

> *Pittsburg &c Ry.* v *Glinn,* 219 Fed. 148.

YARD CLERK, checking cars, not connected with interstate train, excluded.

Pecos & Ry. Co. v *Rosenbloom,* 177 S. W. 952.

Yard clerk, meeting interstate train, included.

St. Louis &c Ry. v *Seale,* 229 U. S. 156; 33 S. C. 651; 59 L. Ed. 1139; rev. 148 S. W. 1099.

SECTION FOREMAN, of switch yard, where interstate train made up, included.

Willever v *Delaware &c R. R.,* 94 Atl. 595.

Section foreman, helping his crew to lift hand car from track, for mixed interstate and intra-state train, included.

Texas &c Ry. v *White,* 177 S. W. 1185.

Section foreman injured through negligent operation of interstate freight train included.

Louisville &c Ry. v *Kemp,* 140 Ga. 657; 79 S. E. 558.

INSPECTOR, helping to clear a yard wreck, included.

Southern Ry. v *Puckett,* 85 S. E. 809.

ROUNDHOUSE EMPLOYE, held included.
> *Cross* v *Chicago &c Ry.,* 177 S. W. 1127.

SIGNALMAN: An electric signalman, controlling both inter and intra-state trains, included.
> *Cincinnati &c Ry.* v *Bonham,* 130 Tenn. 435; 171
> ·   S. W. 79.

TRUCK MAN, wheeling interstate freight from warehouse into car, included.
> *Illinois Central R. R.* v *Porter,* 207 Fed. 311.

FLAGMAN at crossing, held excluded.
> *Louisville &c Ry.* v *Barrett,* 85 S. E. 923.

HOSTLER, in yards, dispatching engine, excluded.
> *Gray* v *Chicago & N. W. R. R.,* 153 Wis. 637; 142
> N. W. 505.

Hostler's helper, included.
> *Texas &c Ry.* v *Harvey,* 228 U. S. 319; 33 S. C.
> 518.

PUMPER, at station pump for interstate locomotives, included.
> *Horton* v *Oregon &c Ry.,* 72 Wash. 503, 130 P.
> 897.

EMPTY CARS:

"The hauling of empty freight cars from one state to another, is, in our opinion, interstate commerce within the meaning of the Act."

North Carolina R. R. v *Zachary,* 232 U. S. 248.

"In the very nature of the business, these empty cars must be returned, in order to carry the remaining freight and passengers not able or ready to go at an earlier date, and to accommodate the ordinary traffic in ordinary seasons."

Thompson v *Wabash R. R.,* Mo. 1914; 171 S. W. Rep. 364.

St. Louis &c Ry. v *Anderson,* 173 S. W. 834.

Moved within state, from another state, excluded.

Penna R. R. Co. v *Knox,* 218 Fed. 748; 134 C. C. A. 426.

Employee, assisting in running train, when any cars go outside of state, though employe is not intending to pass state line, included.

Mattocks v *Chicago & A. R. R.,* 187 Ill. App. 529.

Employe on train without interstate passengers, excluded.

Erie R. R. v *Jacobus,* 221 Fed. 335.

Work in part inter- and in part intra-state traffic.
Employe, injured while on local work, excluded.

> *Southern Ry.* v *Murphy,* 70 S. E. 97.

If injured at moment when service is part of interstate commerce, included.

> *Corbett* v *Boston &c R. R.,* 219 Mass. 351; 107
> N. E. 60.

Handling both inter- and intra-state freight cars just
prior to injury, included.

> *Pittsburg &c Ry.* v *Glinn,* 135 C. C. A. 46; 219
> Fed. 148.

Test is whether the particular work at the time of
injury was so closely connected with interstate traffic as
to be part thereof.

> *Eng* v *Southern Pac. R. R.,* 210 Fed. 92.

Fireman, working on intra-state train, ordinarily employed in interstate traffic, included.

> *Behrens* v *Illinois Central R. R.,* 192 Fed. 581.

GOING TO WORK. Reporting for interstate duty at station on express order, included.

> *Lamphere* v *Oregon R. & N. Co.*, 196 Fed. 336; rev. 193 Fed. 248.

Going to work on switch engine, used at outset of shift in interstate commerce, included.

> *Knowles* v *New York &c R. R.*, 150 N. Y. S. 99; 164 App. Div. 711.

GOING HOME. Engineer, going home on push car, included.

> *Louisville &c R. R.* v *Walker*, 162 Ky. 299; 172 S. W. 517.

Section hand, returning on hand car to camp, and also to a point where hand car was to be removed from track, included.

> *San Pedro &c Ry.* v *Davids*, 210 Fed. 870.

Employe riding on a train to his home, and killed in collision, held excluded.

> *Bennett* v *Lehigh Valley R. R.*, 197 Fed. 578.

Pumper, going home on hand car, included.

> *Horton* v *Oregon &c Ry.*, 72 Wash. 503; 130 Pac. 897.

TEMPORARY ABSENCE: When Act excludes.

Taher v *Dulleth,* 150 N. W. 489.

Laborer on work-train, boarding freight train to get mail, excluded.

Meyers v *Norfolk Ry.,* 78 S. E. 280.

Employe, going to roundhouse for his own purpose, excluded.

Padgett v *Seaboard Air Line,* 99 S. C. 364; 83
S. E. 633; Aff. 236 U. S. 668; 35 S. C. 481.

Going from saloon to station for orders after brief absence, included.

Graber v *Duluth &c R. R.,* 159 Wis., 414; 150
N. W. 489.

LOADING AND UNLOADING. Unloading steel rails after reaching their destination, excluded.

Pierson v *New York &c R. R.,* 85 Atl. 233.

TRACK REPAIRS; relaying track for interstate and intra-state trains, excluded.

Charleston &c Ry. v *Anchors,* 73 S. E. 551.

Laborer working on track over which interstate trains have not yet run, excluded.

Chicago &c R. R. v *Steele,* 108 N. E. 4.

Section hand, engaged in ballasting main track, carrying interstate passengers and freight, included.

San Pedro &c Ry. v *Davids,* 210 Fed. 870.

Repairing sidetrack for interstate traffic, included.

Clark v *Chicago Gt. W. R. R.,* 152 N. W. 635.

Shoveling dirt from between interstate tracks, included.

Lombardo v *Boston &c R. R.,* 223 Fed. 427.

Laborer on trestle, used in interstate commerce, walking on tracks to boarding-house, included.

Louisville &c Ry. v *Walkers' Admr.,* 162 Ky. 209; 172 S. W. 517.

Waiting for train to pass over track used for interstate traffic, on which laborer was repairing rails, included.

Glunt v *Penna. R. R.,* 95 Atl. 109.

MOVING MATERIAL: Carrying material to repair bridge, used in both interstate and intra-state traffic, included.

> *Pederson* v *Delaware &c Ry.,* 229 U. S. 146; 33 S. C. 648; 57 L. Ed. 1125; rev. 117 C. C. A. 33; 197 Fed. 537.

Hauling coal, which might be used on interstate trains, excluded.

> *Barker* v *Kansas City &c Ry.,* 94 Kans. 176; 146 Pac. 358.

Moving coal or water from one state to another for interstate traffic use, included.

> *Barker* v *Kansas City &c Ry.,* 88 Kans. 767; 129 Pac. 1151.

Unloading coal from cars, held included.

> *Kamboris* v *Oregon & W. R. & N. Co.,* 146 Pac. 1097.

Switching coal cars from another state to trestle for unloading, included.

> *Barlow* v *Lehigh Valley R. R.,* 214 N. Y. 116; 107 N. E. 814; Aff. 143 N. Y. S. 1053; 158 App. Div. 768.

MINING COAL, excluded.

> *Delaware &c Ry.* v *Yurkonis,* 220 Fed. 429; Aff.
> 213 Fed. 537; App. Dis. 238 U. S. 439; 35
> S. C. 902.

> *Boyle* v *Penna R. R.,* 221 Fed. 453.

"The mere fact that the coal might be or was intended to be used in the conduct of interstate commerce after it was mined and transported did not make the injury one received by the plaintiff while he was engaged in interstate commerce."

> *Delaware, L. & W. R. R.* v *Yurkonis,* 238 U. S.
> 439; Dism. Writ 220 Fed. 429.

BRIDGE WORK; employe working on a bridge or cut-off not yet provided with rails, excluded.

> *Bravis* v *Chicago &c Ry.,* 217 Fed. 234; 133 C. C.
> A. 228.

Workman on temporary bridge, over which railroad intended running interstate trains, included.

> *Columbia &c Ry.* v *Sauter,* 223 Fed. 604.

Repairing bridge on interstate line, included.

> *Thomson* v *Columbia &c Ry.,* 205 Fed. 203.

STEAM SHOVEL; engineer operating on interstate road, included.

> *Fralich* v *Chicago &c Ry.,* 217 Fed. 675.

Weighing; a member of a train crew, weighing cars after delivery to consignee of inter-state freight, to determine net weight, included.

> *Wheeling Terminal R. R.* v *Russell,* 209 Fed.
> 795; 126 C. C. A. 519.

48

TEARING DOWN STRUCTURE, that a new one could be constructed for interstate business, excluded.

> *Thomas* v *Boston & Maine R. R.,* 218 Fed. 143; judgment reversed 219 Fed. 180; 134 C. C. A. 554.

BUILDING STRUCTURE, or construction of instrumentality intended to be used in interstate commerce, excluded.

> *Brans* v *Chicago &c R. R.,* 217 F. 234.

Building coal chute, excluded.

> *Voris* v *Chicago &c Ry.,* 172 Mo. App. 125, 157 S. W. 835.

Framing a new office in freight shed, used for both inter- and intra-state traffic, included.

> *Eng* v *Southern Pacific Ry.,* 210 F. 92.

Constructing tunnel, excluded.

> *Jackson* v *Chicago &c Ry.,* 210 F. 495.

STREET RAILWAYS; servants in charge of street car operating within state, excluded.

> *Kiser* v *Metropolitan St. Ry.,* 175 S. W. 98.

Where street railway traffic is interstate, employes included.

> *South Covington &c Ry.* v *City of Covington,* 35 Sup. Ct. 158; rev. 146 Ky. 592; 143 S. W. 78.

BOATS; tug boat of railroad, included.

> *Erie R. R.* v *Jacobus,* 221 Fed. 335.

Hauling logs to seaport within state, excluded.

> *Bay* v *Merrill & Ring L. Co.,* 220 Fed. 295; Aff. 211 Fed. 717.

IN TRANSIT; passing from one point to another within state, through another state, included.

> *Louisville &c Ry.* v *Allen,* 152 Ky. 145; 153 S. W. 198; reh. over. 152 Ky. 837; 154 S. W. 371.

INSTRUMENTALITIES; all employees who participate in the maintenance or operation of instrumentalities for general use of an interstate railroad are included.

> *Montgomery* v *Southern Pac. Co.*, 131 Pac. 507.
>
> *Eng* v *Southern Pac. Ry.*, 210 Fed. 92.

Disconnecting steampipe on interstate train, included.

> *Kansas City S. Ry.* v *Miller*, 175 S. W. 1164.

Installing block signal system on track over which interstate trains passed, included.

> *Saunders* v *Southern Ry.*, 167 N. C. 375; 83 S. E. 573.

Section hand, repairing switch so as not to delay interstate traffic, included.

> *Jones* v *Chesapeake &c Ry.*, 149 Ky. 566; 149 S. W. 95.

Employee, working on switch mechanism and struck by intra-state train, excluded.

> *Granger* v *Penna. R. R.*, 86 Atl. 264.

Supplying ice to interstate train, included.

> *Freeman* v *Powell*, 144 S. W. 1033; 148 S. W. 290.

"All employes who participate in the maintenance or operation of the instrumentalities for the general use of an interstate commerce railroad, thereby enhancing the utility of such commerce, are necessarily engaged in the work of interstate commerce, within the meaning of the Act. The fact that a portion of plaintiff's work pertained to local traffic would not change the character of his labor in the performance of acts reasonably proximate and essential to the moving of interstate freight and and in assistance thereof."

> *Montgomery* v *Southern Pac. Co.*, 64 Oregon 597; 131 Pac. 507.

Moving oil from oil car to provide fuel for engines, included. *Ib.*

ENGINE REPAIR; boilermaker's helper, injured while assisting in shops in repairing an engine, regularly in use in interstate commerce, included.

> *Law* v *Illinois Central R. R.,* 208 Fed. 869; 126 C. C. A. 27.

Machinist in yards, sent to repair switch engine handling interstate freight, included.

> *Staley* v *Illinois C. R. R.,* 109 N. E. 342.

Repairing switch engine for mixed traffic, temporarily withdrawn, included.

> *Southern Pac. Ry.* v *Pillsbury,* 151 Pac. 277.

Mechanic in repair shop, excluded.

> *Shanks* v *Delaware &c Ry.,* 214 N. Y. 416; 108 N. E. 644.

Car diverted for necessary repair held included.

> *St. Louis &c Ry.* v *Conarty,* 155 S. W. 93.

Repairing car of another railroad company, excluded.

> *Heimbach* v *Lehigh Valley R. R.,* 197 Fed. 579.

Repairing boiler of wrecking train engine lying in roundhouse, excluded, it being an appliance which may or may not be used in interstate commerce.

> *Ruck* v *Chicago &c Ry.,* 153 Wis. 158; 140 N. W. 1074.

CLEANING STENCILS, excluded.

> *Illinois C. R. R.* v *Rogers,* 221 Fed.. 52; C. C. A.

QUESTION FOR JURY: Whether employe was at the time engaged in interstate passenger or freight traffic, is a question of fact to be determined by the jury.

Southern Pacific Co. v *Vaugh*, 165 S. W. 885.

North Carolina R. R. v *Zachary*, 232 U. S. 248.

If right to submit question to jury be denied, Supreme Court will analyze evidence.

North Carolina R. R. v *Zachary*, 232 U. S. 248.

Southern Pac. Co. v *Schuyler*, 227 U. S. 601.

Instruction that engineer was engaged in interstate commerce held correct.

Louisville &c R. v *Holloway's Admr.*, 163 Ky. 125; 173 S. W. 343.

General verdict will not be sustained when contrary to special finding that plaintiff was not engaged in interstate commerce.

Barber v *Kansas City &c Ry.*, 94 Kan. 176; 146 Pac. 358.

Interstate Commerce—Agent or instrument causing injury need not be engaged in—

Act does not require that a fellow-servant, whose negligence causes injury, shall be engaged in interstate commerce.

Pedersen v *Delaware &c R. R.*, 229 U. S. 146.
Second Employers' Liability Cases, 223 U. S. 1.
Louisville &c Ry. v *Walkers' Admr.*, 162 Ky. 209; 172 S. W. 517.
Northern Pac. Ry. v *Maerkl*, 198 Fed. 1; 117 C. C. A. 237.

"It is not essential, where the causal negligence is that of a co-employe, that he also be employed in interstate commerce, for, if the other conditions be present, the statute gives a right of recovery for injury or death resulting from the negligence 'of any of the * * employes of such carrier,' and this includes an employe engaged in interstate commerce."

Pedersen v *Delaware &c R. R.*, 229 U. S. 146.   .
Second Employers' Liability Cases, 223 U. S. 1, 51.

Act is applicable although the train, engine, car or instrumentality, causing the injury, was not used in interstate commerce. Engineer injured by intra-state locomotive may recover.

Pittsburgh &c Ry. v *Farmers &c Trust Co.*, 108 N. E. 108.

Recovery may be had although the injury resulted from a defective brake step on an intra-state car.

Crandall v *Chicago & G. W. Ry.*, 127 Minn. 498; 150 N. W. 165.

Dead engine hauled by interstate train—see:

Atlantic Coast Line v *Jones*, 9 Ala. App. 499; 63 So. 693.

Employer and Employee—Relation must exist.

Act gives no right of recovery to a **Pullman car porter**, not being an "employe" of the railroad.

"We are of the opinion that Congress used the words 'employe' and 'employed' in the statute in their natural sense, and intended to describe the conventional relation of employer and employe. It was well known that there were on inter-state trains persons engaged in various services for other masters. Congress, familiar with this situation, did not use any appropriate expression which could be undertaken to indicate a purpose to include such persons among those to whom the railroad company was to be liable under the Act."

Robinson v *Baltimore & Ohio Railroad Co.,* 237 U. S. 84; Aff. 40 App. D. C. 169, (1915).

Cincinnati &c Ry. v *Swamis Admr.,* 160 Ky. 458; 169 S. W. 889.

Act renders **Lessor Railroad** of its entire intra-state line liable for interstate lessee's negligence, when lessor is responsible by local law.

> *Northern Pac. R. R.* v *Zachary,* 232 U. S. 248; 34 S. C. 305; Rev. 156 N. C. 496.

Lessor railroad is not liable to employe of lessee.

> *Wagner* v *Chicago &c R. R.,* 265 Ill. 245; 109 N. E. 809; Aff. 180 Ill. App. 196.
> *Campbell* v *Canadian Northern Ry.,* 124 Minn. 245; 144 N. W. 772.

Leased and joint railroads must use ordinary care to maintain tracks in safe condition for employes of each other.

> *Chicago &c R. R.* v *Denius,* 103 N. E. 652.

Railroad is liable for defects in track operated under **traffic arrangements.**

> *Campbell* v *Canadian Northern Ry.,* 124 Minn. 245; 144 N. W. 772.

EXPRESS AGENT cannot hold railroad.

> *Atlantic Coast Line* v *Whitney,* 63 Fla. 124; 56 So. 937.

Relation of master and servant exists when employe, engaged in relaying rails, is asleep at night in shanty car on side track.

> *Sandors* v *Charleston &c R. R.,* 97 S. C. 50; 81 S. C. 283.

Relation does not exist when employe is going home.

> *Dodge* v *Chicago &c R. R.,* 146 N. W. 14.

Negligence—Employer must be guilty of—

"Plainly, it was the intention of Congress to base the action upon negligence only, and to exclude responsibility of the carrier to its employes for defects and insufficiencies not attributable to negligence. The common law rule is that an employer is not a guarantor of the safety of the place of work or of the machinery and appliances of the work; the extent of its duty to its employes is to see that ordinary care and prudence are exercised, to the end that the place in which the work is to be performed and the tools and appliances of the work may be safe for the workman."

Seaboard Air Line v *Horton*, 233 U. S. 492.

Plaintiff must allege and prove negligence of railroad's agents or servants or defects of appliances.

Baltimore &c R. R. v *Whitacre*, 124 Md. 411; 92 Atl. 1060.

Negligence of railroad in failing to discharge some duty owed the employe under the statutes or the common law of master and servant must be shown.

Cincinnati &c Ry. v *Swarm's Admr.*, 160 Ky. 458; 169 S. W. 886.

As to railroad's negligence, the laws of the state may be looked to. *Ib.*

The common law of the state where accident occurred determines whether act complained of amounts to negligence.

Helm v *Cincinnati &c Ry.*, 156 Ky. 240; 160 S. W. 945.

QUESTION FOR JURY: Whether carrier was negligent in permitting low places in track, causing engine to lurch, is question for jury.

> *Louisville &c Ry.* v *Lankford,* 209 Fed. 321; 126 C. C. A. 277.

So, as to permitting runaway of car.

> *Penna R. R.* v *Hickey,* 210 Fed. 786.

So, as to using road engine, instead of one with front foot board.

> *Louisville &c R. R.* v *Lankford,* 209 Fed. 321; 126 C. C. A. 247.

Evidence of negligence, held sufficient for submitting to jury.

> *North Carolina R. R.* v *Zachary,,* 232 U. S. 248; 34 S. C. 305; Rev. 156 N. C. 496.

Failure to properly light and guard: Question is for jury.

> *Copper River R. R.* v *Heney,* 211 Fed. 459.

So, whether automatic coupler was in workable condition.

> *Nashville &c Ry.* v *Heney,* 158 Ky. 88; 164 S. W. 310.

> *See: Smith* v *Atlantic Coast Line R. R.,* 210 Fed. 761.

Where railroad's negligence depends on the reasonableness of a switch yard rule and the facts are in dispute, the court should instruct the jury when rule would be reasonable.

> *Wright* v *Chicago &c Ry.,* 146 N. W. 1024; Aff. 143 N. W. 220; 94 Neb. 317.

Negligence—Of employee—Only diminishes damages—

"This statute rejects the common law rule, that contributory negligence is a complete bar or defense, and adopts another, being deemed more reasonable. This provision means, and can only mean, that where the causal negligence is attributable partly to the carrier and partly to the injured employe, he shall not recover full damages, but only a diminished sum bearing the same relation to the full damages that the negligence attributable to the carrier bears to the negligence attributable to both, the purpose being to exclude from the recovery a proportional part of the damages corresponding to the employe's contribution to the total negligence."

Seaboard Air Line Railway v Tilghman, 237 U.
S. 499; Rev. 167 N. C. 163.

"The statutory direction that the diminution shall be "in proportion to the amount of negligence attributable to such employe" means and can only mean, that where the causal negligence is partly attributable to him and partly to the carrier, he shall not recover full damages but only a proportional amount, bearing the same relation to the full amount as the negligence attributable to the carrier bears to the entire negligence attributable to both; the purpose being to abrogate the common law rule completely exonerating the carrier from liability in such a case, and to substitute a new rule confining the exoneration to a proportional amount of the damages corresponding to the amount of negligence attributable to the employe."

Norfolk &c Ry. v Earnest, 229 U. S. 114; 33 S.
C. 654; 57 L. Ed. 1096.

Second Employers' Liability Cases, 223 U. S. 1.

Grand Trunk Western Ry. v Lindsay, 233 U. S.
42.

Nashville &c Ry. v Banks, 156 Ky. 609; 161 S.
W. 554.

Pfeiffer v Oregon &c Co., 144 Pac. 762.

Instruction to diminish damages in proportion to employe's negligence is not affirmatively error.

St. Louis &c R. R. v Vernon, 161 S. W. 84.

Recovery should not be diminished in proportion to the amount of employe's negligence.

Nashville &c Ry. v Henry, 158 Ky. 88; 164 S. W.
310.

Contributory negligence does not entirely bar recovery, when negligence of railroad also caused injury.

> *Baltimore &c R. R.* v *Whitren,* 124 Md. 411; 92
> A. 1060.
> *Louisville &c R. R.* v *Heinings Admr.,* 162 Ky.
> 14; 171 S. W. 853.
> *Ryan* v *Manhattan &c Co.,* 145 Pac. 907.
> *Fish* v *Chicago &c R. R.,* 172 S. W. 340.
> *Sounders* v *Southern R. R.,* 167 N. C. 375; 83 S.
> E. 573.
> *Chadwick* v *Oregon, Wash. &c Co.,* 144 Pac. 1165.

Contributory negligence goes to diminution of damages only.

> *Hackney* v *Missouri &c Ry.,* 149 Pac. 421.
> *Pankey* v *Atchison &c R. R.,* 180 Mo. App. 185;
> 168 S. W. 274.

Jury must apportion amount of diminution.

> *Hackney* v *Missouri &c Ry.,* 149 Pac. 421.

Instruction, allowing recovery without proof of railroad's negligence, error.

> *Louisville &c R. R.* v *Holloway's Admr.,* 163 Ky.
> 125; 173 S. W. 343.

Comparative and preponderance of negligence, see:

> *Wiles* v *Great Northern Ry.,* 125 Minn. 348; 147
> N. W. 427.
> *New York &c R. R.* v *Niebel,* 214 F. 952.

Contributory negligence does not authorize charge to find for railroad.

> *Chicago & Great West. R. R.* v *McCormick,* 200
> F. 357; 118 C. C. A. 527.

Nor bar recovery, no matter how gross in degree or proximate a cause.

> *Pennsylvania R. R.* v *Cole,* 214 F. 948.
> *New York &c R. R.* v *Niebel,* 214 F. 952.

Plaintiff need not show he was free from fault, this merely reducing damages.

> *Charleston &c R. R.* v *Brown,* 79 S. E. 932.

Contributory negligence only reduces damages.

> *White* v *Central Vermont Ry.,* 89 Atl. 618.
> *McDonald* v *Railway Transfer Co.,* 141 N. W. 177.
> *Hardwick* v *Wabash R. R.,* 181 Mo. App. 156; 168 S. W. 328.
> *Lloyd* v *Southern Ry.,* 166 N. C. 24; 81 S. E. 1003.

Instruction should charge that it is employe's duty to perform his duties in a reasonably safe way and exercise the care of an ordinarily prudent person under like circumstances.

> *Nashville &c Ry.* v *Banks,* 156 Ky. 609; 161 S. W. 554.

Only such contributory negligence as proximately contributed to the injury can be considered in reduction of damages.

> *Illinois Central R. R.* v *Porter,* 207 F. 311; 125 C. C. A. 55.

Contributory negligence must be proved by railroad.

> *White* v *Central Vermont R. R.,* 89 Atl. 618.

Extent of reduction of damages is for jury.

> *Louisville &c R. R.* v *Fleming,* 69 So. 125.
> *Kenney* v *Seaboard Air Line Ry.,* 165 N. C. 99; 80 S. E. 1078.

Act establishes rule of comparative negligence.

> *Grand Trunk R. R.* v *Lindsay,* 233 U. S. 42; 34 S. C. 581; Aff. 201 F. 836; 120 C. C. A. 166.

Instruction limiting plaintiff's knowledge of location and construction of a trestle to actual knowledge, held not objectionable.

> *Missouri &c Ry.* v *Bunkley,* 153 S. W. 937.

Rule as to contributory negligence applies to all grades of carelessness, whether slight or gross.

Mississippi Central R. R. v *Robinson,* 64 So. 838.

Instruction that act of switchman in riding on pilot with knowledge of danger should reduce damages to nominal sum, error.

Louisville &c R. R. v *Lankford,* 209 F. 321; 126
C. C. A. 247.

Contributory negligence must be pleaded and proved by defendant, if so required by local procedure.

Seaboard Air Line Ry. v *Moore,* 228 U. S. 433;
33 S. C. 580; 57 L. Ed. 907; Aff. 193 F. 1022;
113 C. C. A. 668.

Fleming v *Norfolk &c Ry.,* (*N. Car.*) 76 S. E.
212.

INSTRUCTION should construe act in application to facts.

> *Pelton* v *Illinois Central R. R.,* 150 N. W. 236; reh. den. 153 N. W. 334.

Contributory negligence: Instruction held correct.

> *Walsh* v *Lake Shore &c Ry.,* 151 N. W. 754.
>
> *Pittsburgh &c Ry.* v *Farmers &c Co.,* 108 N. E. 108.

Erroneous: *Penna Ry.* v *Sheeley,* 221 F. 901.

Instruction of law as to acts of engineer in emergency held correct.

> *Louisville &c R. R.* v *Holloway's Admr.,* 163 Ky. 125; 173 S. W. 343.

Instruction that if the jury found that plaintiff did a certain act, such act was the proximate cause, and he could not recover, error.

> *Grand Trunk Ry.* v *Lindsay,* 201 F. 36; 120 C. C. A. 166.

Carrier is entitled to concrete instruction as to contributory negligence.

> *Illinois Central R. R.* v *Nelson,* 203 F. 956; 122 C. C. A. 258.

The fact that the employe's negligence was equal to or greater than the carrier's, does not wholly bar recovery.

> *Louisville &c R. R.* v *Wene,* 202 F. 887; 121 C. C. A. 245.

Instruction as to proportionate care, held not error.

> *St. Louis &c Ry.* v *Rodgers,* 176 S. W. 696.

Evidence as to dangerous proximity of switch handle to cars, is admissible and rebuttable by proof of warning.

> *McDonald* v *Railway Transfer Co.,* 141 N. W. 177.

Negligence—Employer is liable for fellow-servant's.

Fellow servant rule, abolished by act.

> *Carter* v *Kansas City &c R. R.*, 155 S. W. 638.
>
> *Louisville &c R. R.* v *Heinig's Admr.*, 162 Ky. 14; 171 S. W. 853.

Negligence of a flagman in failing to protect rear of a freight conductor's train, whereby the latter is injured, is that of the railroad.

> *Penna R. R.* v *Goughnor*, 208 F. 961; 126 C. C. A. 39.

A brakeman held entitled to rely on another brakeman's statement that an engine could pass cars on another track without his being caught.

> *Skoggs* v *Illinois Central R. R.*, 124 Minn. 503; 145 N. W. 381.

Failure of an engineer fellow servant to discover an open switch, left open by another company, does not relieve carrier.

> *Campbell* v *Canadian N. Ry.*, 124 Minn. 245; 144 N. W. 772.

Assumption of Risk—Common law defence remains.

"The defense of assumption of risk remains as at common law, saving in the cases mentioned in § 4."

Southern Ry. v *Crockett*, 234 U. S. 725.

Seaboard Air Line v *Horton*, 233 U. S. 492.

"It seems to us that Section 4 in eliminating the defense of assumption of risk in the cases indicated quite plainly evidences the legislative intent that in all other cases such assumption shall have its former effect as a complete bar to the action. And, taking Sections 3 and 4 together, there is no doubt that Congress recognized the distinction between contributory negligence and assumption of risk, for, while it is declared that neither of these shall avail the carrier in cases where the violation of a statute has contributed to the injury or death of the employe, there is, with respect to cases not in this category, a limitation upon the effect that is to be given to contributory negligence, while no corresponding limitation is imposed upon the defence of assumption of risk; perhaps none was feasible."

Seaboard Air Line v *Horton*, 233 U. S. 492; 34 S. C. 635; 58 L. E. 1062.

Southern Ry. v *Howerton*, Ind. 1914, 106 N. E. Rep. 369.

"Upon the merits, we, of course, sustain the contention that by the Act the defense of assumption of risk remains as at common law, saving in the cases mentioned in Section 4; that is to say, any case where the violation by such common carrier of any statute enacted for the safety of employes contributed to the injury or death of such employe."

Southern Ry. v *Crockett*, 234 U. S. 725; 34 S. C. 897.

"The very recent case of *Seaboard Air Line* v *Horton* (1914), 233 U. S. 492, 34 S. C. 635, 58 L. Ed. —, goes still farther in holding that the statute referred to in Sections 3 and 4 of the Act means only federal statutes, so that under that and prior decisions assumption of risk remains as before, except as modified by the application of Section 4 to federal statutes, and that the common law still obtains with respect to assumption of risk from defective appliances, while abrogating the fellow servant rule of the common law."

Southern Ry. v *Howerton*, Ind. 1914, 105 N. E. Rep. 1025.

Defense of assumption of risk is not eliminated, except where the injury has happened on account of the violation of some federal statute designed for the protection of the employe.

> *Oberlin* v *Oregon &c Co.,* 71 Or. 177; 142 Pac. 554.
>
> *Horton* v *Seaboard Air Line Ry.,* 162 N. C. 424; 78 S. E. 494.
>
> *Freeman* v *Powell* (Tex. Civ. App.), 144 S. W. 1033.
>
> *Neil* v *Idaho &c Ry.,* 22 Idaho 74; 125 Pac. 331.
>
> *Barker* v *Kansas City &c Ry.,* 88 Kan. 767; 129 Pac. 1151; 43 L. R. A. (N. S. 1121).

Doctrine of assumed risk remains as before at common law, save in exceptions stated, where violation of federal safety acts contributed to injury.

> *Southern Ry.* v *Howerton,* 105 N. E. Rep. 1025; 106 N. E. 369.
>
> *Hall* v *Vandalia R. R.,* 169 Ill. App. 12.
>
> *Kendrick* v *Chicago &c Ry.,* 188 Ill. App. 172.
>
> *Devine* v *Chicago &c R. R.,* 185 Ill. App. 488; Aff. 266 Ill. 248; 107 N. E. 595.
>
> *Truesdell* v *Chesapeake &c R. R.,* 159 Ky. 918; 169 S. W. 471.

Risk is not assumed by engineer of railroad's negligence in leaving car on siding within striking distance.

> *Wright* v *Yazoo &c R. R.,* 197 Fed. 94.

Risk is not assumed of injury from railroad's negligence.

> *Hawkins* v *St. Louis &c Ry.,* 174 S. W. Rep. 129.
>
> *Thornton* v *Seaboard Air Line,* 98 S. Car. 348; 82 S. E. 423.

Where risks from railroad's negligence are not assumed under state law, question held immaterial.

> *Cross* v *Chicago &c Ry.,* 177 S. W. Rep. 1123.

Defense of assumed risk is available in cases not within exception of act.

> *Columbia &c R. R.* v *Sauter*, 223 F. 604.
> *Fish* v *Chicago, Rock &c R. R.*, 172 S. W. 340.
> *Barker* v *Kansas City &c Ry.*, 88 Kans. 767; 129
>   P. 1151; 43 L. R. A. (N. S.) 1121.
> *Guana* v *Southern Pac. Co.*, 139 Pac. 782.

Act does not abolish defense of assumed risk where the master breaks a common law duty, as distinguished from the specified statutory duty.

> *New York &c R. R.* v *Vizzari*, 210 F. 118; 126 C.
>   C. A. 632.

Act overcomes provisions of State constitutions as to assumed risk.

> *Bramlett* v *Southern Ry.*, 98 S. C. 319; 82 S. E.
>   501.

Track walker assumes risk from trains properly operated.

> *Connelly* v *Penna R. R.*, 201 F. 54; 119 C. C. A.
>   392.

Instructions as to assumed risk held proper.

> *Nashville &c R. R.* v *Henry*, 158 Ky. 88; 164 S.
>   W. 310.

Doctrine of assumption of risk is not applicable in regard to defective condition of tracks, causing cars to become uncoupled.

> *Hayes* v *Wabash R. R.*, 180 Ill. App. 511.

Risk of negligence of his flagman is not assumed by conductor.

> *Penna. R. R.* v *Goughnor*, 208 F. 961; 126 C. C.
>   A. 39.

Assumption of risk is no defense in action by switchman, where engineer stopped train with a jerk.

> *La Mere* v *Railway Transfer Co.*, 145 N. W.
>   1068.

Interstate commerce Act makes no change in rule except as to safety appliances.

Glenn v *Cincinnati &c Ry.*, 157 Ky. 453; 163 S. W. 461.

La Mere v *Railway Transfer Co.*, 145 N. W. 1068.

Assumption of risk is no defense where the railroad has violated a state law prohibiting extra hazardous employment.

Opsahl v *Northern P. R. R.*, 78 Wash. 197; 138 P. 681.

Brakeman, held not to have assumed risk of injury from conductor's negligence in inspecting manner of loading on a flat car.

Michigan C. R. R. v *Schaffer*, 220 F. 809.

Risk is not assumed of danger from injury by side-tracked cars moving down grade with unset brakes.

Illinois C. R. R. v *Stewart*, 223 F. 30.

Risk of injury is not assumed by section hand because an insufficient number of men were ordered to remove a motor car from track.

Missouri &c Ry. v *Freeman*, 168 S. W. 69.

Risk is not assumed by engineer from negligent adjustment of lever of ash pan just from repair shop.

Lloyd v *Southern Ry.*, 166 N. C. 24; 81 S. E. 1003.

Assumed risk distinguished from contributory negligence, the one barring, the other only diminishing recovery.

Chesapeake &c Ry. v *DeAtley*, 159 Ky. 718; 169 S. W. 471.

Risk held assumed from tracks having been constructed too close together.

Kirbo v *Southern Ry.*, 84 S. E. 491.

Finding that yard conductor had assumed risk of negligent operation of cars running by gravity, held justified, and instruction that risks incident to negligence of railroad officers were not assumed, properly denied.

Boldt v *Penna. R. R.*, 218 F. 367; 134 C. C. A. 175.

Assumption of risk is a question for jury.

McGovern v *Phila. R. R.*, 235 U. S. 389.

Defense of assumed risk may be made, though contrary to state statute.

Texas &c Ry. v *White*, 177 S. W. 1185.

A roundhouse foreman who stumbled over a jack and fell under a locomotive held not to have assumed the risk as matter of law, though he knew the insufficiency of lights.

Hawkins v *St. Louis &c R. R.*, 174 S. W. 129.

INSTRUCTION that if a person of ordinary care would have continued in the service with knowledge of a defect, the injured employe did not assume the risk, error.

Galveston &c Ry. v *Hodnett*, 163 S. W. 13; Rev'g 155 S. W. 678.

Refusal to direct verdict because of assumed risk, upheld.

Erie R. R. v *Jacobus*, 221 F. 335.

Instruction which fails to except from risks assumed those resulting from the railroad's negligence, error.

Houston &c Ry. v *Menefee*, 162 S. W. 1038.

Assumption of Risk—Distinguished from contributory negligence.

"Contributory negligence involves the notion of some fault or breach of duty on the part of the employe, and since it is ordinarily his duty to take some precaution for his own safety when engaged in a hazardous occupation, contributory negligence is sometimes defined as a failure to use such care for his safety as ordinarily prudent employes in similar circumstances would use. On the other hand, the assumption of risk, even though the risk be obvious, may be free from any suggestion of fault or negligence on the part of the employe. The risks may be present notwithstanding the exercise of all reasonable care on his part. Some employments are necessarily fraught with danger to the workman—danger that must be and is confronted in the line of duty. Such dangers as are normally and necessarily incident to the occupation are presumably taken into account when fixing the rate of wages. And a workman of mature years is taken to assume risks of this sort, whether he is actually aware of them or not. But risks of another sort, not naturally incident to the occupation, may arise out of the failure of the employer to exercise due care with respect to providing a safe place to work and suitable and safe appliances for the work. These the employe is not treated as assuming until he becomes aware of the defect or disrepair, and of the risk arising from it, unless defect and risk alike are so obvious that an ordinarily prudent person under the circumstances would have observed and appreciated them. When the employee does know of the defect, and appreciates the risk that is attributable to it, and then if he continues in the employment, without objection, or without obtaining from his employer or his representative an assurance that the defect will be remedied, the employe assumes the risk, even though it arise out of the master's breach of duty. If, however, there be a promise of reparation, then during such time as may be reasonably required for its performance or until the particular time specified for its performance, the employe relying upon the promise does not assume the risk unless at least the danger be so imminent that no ordinarily prudent man under the circumstances would rely upon such promise."

Seaboard Air Line Co. v Horton, 233 U. S. 492.
Gila Valley Ry. Co. v Hall, 232 U. S. 94.
Texas & Ry. v Harvey, 228 U. S. 319.
Clarke v Holmes, 7 Hurl. & Norm. 937.

ASSUMPTION OF RISK—DISTINGUISHED FROM CONTRIBUTORY NEGLIGENCE

Assumption of risk is distinguished from want of care.

"The argument is that even although the engineer did not know of the protruding cars and therefore did not consciously incur the great risk to result from the collision, yet as by proper precaution he could have discovered the fact that the cars were protruding, he must be considered to have assumed the risk which resulted from want of care. But this argument, as well as that he must have known that such danger might arise, has no relation to the doctrine of assumption of the risk and only call for the application of the principle of contributory negligence or of fellow servant."

Yazoo v Mississippi V. R. R., 235 U. S. 376; Aff. 207 F. 281.

"Plaintiff certainly did not assume the risk that the engineer would negligently run the train at a high and dangerous rate of speed, contrary to his duty. If we say that he assumed the risk of his own negligence then we make of no effect the provision of the statute that his contributory negligence shall not bar recovery, but shall only diminish the amount of damages to be awarded. We are therefore, of opinion that there is not in this case any question of assumed risk and that the court therefore properly refused to submit the question of assumed risk to the jury."

Mattocks v Chicago &c Ry., 187 Ill. App. 529.

"The railroad is chargeable with the negligence of the engineer, and the fellow-servant doctrine does not apply. The deceased did not assume the risk occasioned through the negligence of the engineer and such risk or danger could not be termed one of the ordinary risks or dangers of the employment of the deceased switchman."

Devine v Chicago &c Ry., 185 Ill. App. 488.

Instruction in terms of Act, correct.

Devine v Chicago &c Ry., 185 Ill. App. 488.

71

Safety Acts—Violation of—Excludes defences.

"Where the injury has been occasioned in part by the failure of the carrier to comply with the exactions of an Act of Congress enacted to promote the safety of employes, the statute abolishes the defense of contributory negligence, not only as a bar to recovery, but for all purposes."

> *Grand Trunk Ry.* v *Lindsay,* 233 U. S. 42.

Contributory negligence of employe does not diminish damages where any safety act has been violated.

> *Grand Trunk &c R. R.* v *Lindsay,* 233 U. S. 42; 34 S. C. 581; Aff. 201 F. 836; 120 C. C. A. 166.
>
> *Southern Ry.* v *Jacobs,* 81 S. E. 99.
>
> *Thornbro* v *Kansas City &c Ry.,* 91 Kan. 684; 139 P. 410; Aff. 92 Kan. 681; 142 P. 250.

Contributory negligence is no defense when a safety act has been violated, but the fact may be considered in reduction of damages.

> *La Mere* v *Railway Tr. Co.,* 145 N. W. 1068.
>
> *Johnston* v *Chicago &c Ry.,* 164 S. W. 260.

Failure of a brakeman to report defective condition of an automatic coupler is not defense.

> *Nashville &c Ry.* v *Henry,* 158 Ky. 88; 164 S. W. 310.

Evidence as to violation of safety act being proximate cause, held sufficient.

> *La Mere* v *Railway Tr. Co.,* 145 N. W. 1068.

Contributory negligence of employe does not affect amount of recovery where a safety act has been violated.

> *St. Louis &c Ry.* v *Anderson,* 173 S. W. 834.

Where a safety appliance act has been violated, defense of contributory negligence is not available even for reduction of damages.

> *Lucas* v *Peoria &c R. R.*, 171 Ill. App. 1.

Reasonable care does not preclude liability for not keeping proper couplers.

> *St. Louis &c R. R.* v *Conarty*, 155 S. W. 93.
>
> *Thornbro* v *Kansas City R. R.*, 92 Kan. 681; 142 P. 250.
>
> *Gordon* v *New Orleans &c Ry.*, 64 So. 1014.

Contributory negligence does not affect amount of recovery where railroad has failed to provide proper couplers.

> *Burbo* v *Minneapolis &c R. R.*, 141 N. W. 300.

Evidence that an examination made two days after accident disclosed defects of a coupler, admissible.

> *Lucas* v *Peoria &c Ry.*, 171 Ill. App. 1.

Assumption of risk: Defense of is not permitted where a safety act has been violated.

> *Thornbro* v *Kansas City &c Ry.*, 91 Kan. 684; Aff. 92 Kan. 681; 142 P. 250.

Act may modify or abolish rules of law and of courts regarding assumption or risk and contributory negligence.

> *Deibeikis* v *Lint-belt Co.*, 201 Ill. 454; 104 N. E. 211.

Exemption applies with like effect as if promulgated by state law.

> *Hogarty* v *Phila. &c R. R.*, 245 Pa. 443; 91 A. 854.

Express exception, where assumed risk is no defense, shows that in other cases, its effect is to bar.

> *Seaboard Air Line* v *Horton*, 233 U. S. 492; 34 S. C. 635; 58 L. Ed. 1062; rev. 162 N. C. 424; 78 S. E. 494.
>
> *Southern R. R.* v *Crockett*, 234 U. S. 725; 34 S. C. 897; 58 L. E. 1564.

Act is in *pari materia* with safety appliance acts.

> *North Carolina R. R.* v *Zachary*, 232 U. S. 248.

Defects in engines, cars, or appliances render railroad liable.

> *Pfeiffer* v *Oregon &c Co.*, 144 Pac. 762.

Both simple and complex tools must be free from defects.

> *Gerkas* v *Oregon &c Co.*, 146 Pac. 970.

Safety appliances are required for all cars and trains, regardless of for what service they are employed.

> *United States* v *Pere Marquette R. R.*, 211 F. 220.

ELECTRIC CARS: "Engines" and "locomotive engineers" in safety appliance act includes electric motors and motormen.

> *Spokane &c Ry.* v *Campbell*, 217 F. 518; 133 C. C. A. 370.

DUE DILIGENCE of railroad to keep safety appliances in good working order is not sufficient defence.

> *Deck* v *St. Louis &c R. R.*, 220 U. S. 580; 31 S. C. 617; 55 L. Ed. 590; Rev. 86 C. C. A. 95; 158 F. 931; 14 A. & E. Cas. 233.

"In *Grand Trunk Ry.* v *Lindsay*, 233 U. S. 42; 34 S. C. 581; 58 L. Ed, the complaint in one paragraph counted on a violation of the Safety Appliance Act and the Employers' Liability Act, and in the other, solely on the latter act, and the cause was tried and the jury instructed under the Safety Appliance Act. The Circuit Court of Appeals sustained the judgment by applying the provisions of the Employers' Liability Act, and the judgment was affirmed in the Supreme Court on the authority of *Seaboard Air Line Co.* v *Duvall* (1912), 225 U. S. 477."

> *Southern Ry.* v *Howerton*, Ind. 1914; 105 N. E. Rep. 1025.

Safety Acts—Only Federal Statutes.

"By the phrase 'any statute enacted for the safety of employes,' Congress evidently intended Federal Statutes, such as the Safety Appliance Acts (March 2, 1893, c. 196, 27 Stat. 531; March 2, 1903, c. 976, 32 Stat. 943; April 14, 1910, c. 160, 36 Stat. 298; February 17, 1911, c. 103, 36 Stat. 913), and the Hours of Service Act (February 4, 1907, c. 2939, 34 Stat. 1415)."

Seaboard Air Line v *Horton,* 233 U. S. 492, 503.

Lauer v *Northern Pac. R. R.,* 145 Pac. 606.

Federal statutes only are referred to by the term "statutes" in the statutory exceptions of assumption of risk and contributory negligence not being permitted as defences when Safety Acts violated.

Gee v *Lehigh Valley R. R.,* 148 N. Y. S. 882; 163 App. Div. 274.

Violation of **HOURS OF SERVICE ACT** renders railroad liable for injury.

St. Louis &c R. R. v *McWhistler,* 145 Ky. 427; 140 S. W. 672.

Hours of Service Act: Mere violation of, is not sufficient to justify recovery, unless negligence of railroad concurs.

Osborne's Admr. v *Cincinnati &c R. R.,* 158 Ky. 176; 164 S. W. 818.

Construction—Federal decisions govern—

Act must be construed in accord with decisions of Federal Courts as to modes of procedure where they constitute a substantial part of the case.

> *Central Vermont Ry.* v *White,* 238 U. S. 507;
> Aff. 87 Vt. 330.
>
> *Seaboard Air Line Ry.* v *Horton,* 228 U. S. 434.

"The United States Courts have uniformly held that as a matter of general law the burden of proving contributory negligence is on the defendant. Congress evidently intended that this statute should be construed in the light of these and other decisions of the Federal Courts."

> *Central Vermont Ry.* v *White's Admx.,* 238 U.
> S. 507; Aff. 87 Vt. 330.

Act must be construed according to the decisions of the United States Supreme Court.

> *Toledo &c Ry.* v *Slavin,* 236 U. S. 454; 35 S. C.
> 306; Rev. 88 Oh. St. 536; 109 N. E. 1077.
>
> *St. Louis R. R.* v *Hesterly,* 228 U. S. 702; 33 S.
> C. 703; 57 L. Ed. 1031; Rev. 98 Ark. 240;
> 135 S. W. 874.
>
> *McAdow* v *Kansas City W. Ry.,* 164 S. W. 188.
>
> *Nashville &c Ry.* v *Henry,* 158 Ky. 88; 164 S. W.
> 310.
>
> *Cincinnati &c Ry.* v *Nolan,* 161 Ky. 205; 170 S.
> W. 650.
>
> *Kendricks* v *Chicago &c Ry.,* 188 Ill. App. 172.
>
> *Louisville &c R. R.* v *Miller,* 156 Ky. 677; 162 S.
> W. 73.

These are conclusive and exclusive.

> *Montgomery* v *Southern Pac. Ry.,* 64 Or. 597;
> 131 Pac. 507.
>
> *Horton* v *Oregon &c R. & N. Co.,* 72 Wash. 503;
> 130 P. 897.

Federal decisions as to procedure must be followed when substantial part of case is affected.

> *Central Vermont R. R.* v *White,* 238 U. S. 507;
> Aff. 87 Vt. 330.
>
> *Seaboard Air Line Ry.* v *Moon,* 228 U. S. 434.

Construction—Rules of—

Right of action must be determined by the Act.

Peck v *Boston &c Ry.*, 223 F. 448.

Delaware &c Ry. v *Yurkonis,* 220 F. 429.

Molliter v *Wabash R. R.*, 180 Mo. App. 84; 168 S. W. 250.

Fithian v *St. Louis &c Ry.,* 188 F. 842.

Act authorizes action which could be maintained otherwise.

Cory v *Lake Shore &c Ry.,* 208 F. 847.

Jackson Lumber Co. v *Courcey,* 9 Ala. App. 488; 63 So. 749.

Act operates where railroad and employe were engaged in interstate commerce.

Louisville &c Ry. v *Strange's Admx.,* 161 S. W. 239.

Act is not to be extended by implication, being in derogation of common law.

McClaugherty v *Rogue River El. Co.,* 140 Pac. 64.

Act is remedial in character and should be so construed as to prevent the mischief and advance the remedy.

St. Louis &c Ry. v Conley, 187 F. 949; 110 C. C. A. 97.

Act enlarges, but does not abridge, liability, and recovery may be had at common law.

Grow v Oregon &c Ry., 138 Pac. 398.

Statutory remedy may be cumulative and not abrogate common law action.

Hayes v Wabash R. R., 180 Ill. App. 511; Dis. 234 U. S. 86; 34 S. C. 729.

Act is not retroactive.

Winfree v Northern Pac. Ry., 227 U. S. 296; Aff. 97 C. C. A. 392.

"This statute permits recovery in cases where recovery could not be had before, and takes from defendant defenses which formerly were available. * * * Such a statute should not be construed as retrospective. It introduced a new policy and quite radically changed the existing law."

Winfree v Northern Pac. R. R. Co., 227 U. S. 296-302.

Relief granted is governed by rulings of Federal Courts, and remedy is exclusive.

Miller v Kansas City &c Ry., 180 Mo. App. 371; 168 S. W. 336.

Laws of state may be looked to, as to relief.

Hogarty v Philadelphia R. R., 240 Pa. 443; 91 A. 854.

Jurisdiction—State courts have concurrent—

State Courts have concurrent jurisdiction.

>*Corbett* v *Boston &c Ry.*, 219 Mass. 351; 107 N.
>E. 60.
>
>*Kamboris* v *Oregon &c Co.*, 146 Pac. 1097.
>
>*McCullough* v *Chicago &c Ry.*, 142 N. W. 67.
>
>*Southern R. R.* v *Howerton*, 105 N. E. 1025;
>Rev. 101 N. E. 121; Reh. den. 106 N. E. 369.
>
>*Moliter* v *Wabash R. R.*, 180 Mo. App. 84; 168
>S. W. 250.
>
>*Easter* v *Virginia Ry.*, 86 S. E. 37.

Superior Court of Washington has competent jurisdiction.

>*Gibson* v *Bellingham & N. Ry.*, 213 F. 488.

Jurisdiction—Removal of cause prohibited—

"The language of both the amendment and the Judicial Code, Section 28, clearly inhibits removal of a cause arising under this Act from a State Court upon the sole ground of diversity of citizenship. The same decision has been announced frequently by lower Courts."

Kansas City Southern Ry. v *Leslie*, 238 U. S. 599; Rev. 112 Ark. 305: (overruling *Van Brimmer* v *Texas &c Ry.*, 190 F. 394.)

Symonds v *St. Louis &c Ry.*, 192 F. 353.

Strauser v *Chicago &c R. R.*, 193 F. 293.

Saiek v *Penna. R. R.*, 193 F. 303.

Lee v *Toledo &c Ry.*, 193 F. 685.

Ullrich v *New York &c Ry.*, 193 F. 768.

Hulac v *Chicago &c Ry.*, 194 F. 747.

McChesney v *Illinois Central R. R.*, 197 F. 85.

DeAtley v *Chesapeake & Ohio Ry.*, 201 F. 591.

Rice v *Boston & Maine R. R.*, 203 F. 580.

Kelly's Admx. v *Chesapeake & Ohio Ry.*, 201 F. 602.

Teel v *Chesapeake & Ohio Ry.*, 204 F. 918.

Patton v *Cincinnati &c Ry.*, 208 F. 29.

Eng v *Southern Pacific Ry.*, 210 F. 92.

Burnett v *Spokane &c Ry.*, 210 F. 94.

Notwithstanding local prejudice.

Lombardo v *Boston &c R. R.*, 223 F. 427.

Peek v *Boston &c R. R.*, 223 F. 448.

Nor although same count states cause of action under state statute or common law.

Strother v *Union Pac. R. R.*, 220 F. 731. (D. C. Mo.)

"If a cause of action containing all the elements of removability be joined with a count stating a cause of action not originally cognizable in the Federal court, nevertheless the defendant may remove the former cause of action and this will carry the entire case with it." *Ib.*

Where the facts alleged bring the cause of action within the Act, the case is not removable from state court on any ground.

> *Symonds* v *St. Louis &c R. R.*, 192 F. 353.
>
> *Lee* v *Toledo, St. L. &c R. R.*, 193 F. 685.
>
> *Kansas City &c Ry.* v *Leslie*, 112 Ark. 305; 167 S. W. 83; Rev. 35 S. C. 884.
>
> *Hulac* v *Chicago & N. W. R.*, 194 F. 747.
>
> *DeAtley* v *Chesapeake & O. Ry.*, 147 Ky. 315; 144 S. W. 95.
>
> *Lombardo* v *Boston & M. R. R.*, 223 F. 427.

Where cause has been improperly removed, right to have it remanded is not waived by filing reply.

> *Burnett* v *Spokane &c Ry.*, 210 F. 94.

Cause is not removable though diversity of citizenship exists and requisite amount involved.

> *Pankey* v *Atchison &c Ry.*, 180 Mo. App. 185; 168 S. W. 274.
>
> *Peck* v *Boston & M. R. R.*, 223 F. 448.
>
> *Southern Ry.* v *Puckett*, 85 S. E. 809.

Not removable on ground of local influence and prejudice.

> *Strausser* v *Chicago, B. & Q. R. R.*, 193 F. 293.

Nor on ground of different domicile.

> *Jones* v *Kansas City &c Ry.*, 68 So. 401.

When plaintiff bases his action unequivocally on the Act, cause is not removable, even if facts alleged are insufficient.

> *Smith* v *Camas Prairie R. R.*, 216 F. 799.

Cause may not be removed, although the same complaint states cause of action under common law, state statute or Act, after being held a single cause of action.

Rice v *Boston &c Ry.*, 203 F. 580.

Case brought in state court is not removable although it would be otherwise.

Patton v *Cincinnati &c Ry.*, 208 F. 29.

Lloyd v *North Carolina Ry.*, 162 N. C. 485; 78 S. E. 489.

Act is constitutional, although permitting no removal on ground of diversity of citizenship.

Kelly's Admx. v *Chesapeake &c Ry.*, 201 F. 602.

Mandamus for removal, see Ex parte Roe, 234 U. S. 70; 34 S. Ct. 722; 58 L. Ed. 1217.

"It is, of course, difficult and to me impossible to spell out, surmise or guess any good reason for denying to a defendant common carrier engaged in interstate commerce the right to have a case arising under the Act, when diversity of citizenship and requisite amount in controversy, or local prejudice of the extent named, exist, tried in the Federal Court, but Congress has so decreed in plain language and I discover no ground or theory on which the courts can make over the statute referred to."

Lombardo v *Boston &c Ry.*, 223 Fed. 427.

Peck v *Boston &c Ry.*, 223 Fed. 448.

Contra: *Van Brunner* v *Texas &c Ry.*, 190 Fed. 394.

Action—Joinder of, permitted—

State courts have concurrent jurisdiction and action under Act may be joined with one under state liability act.

> *Atlantic Coast Line Ry.* v *Jones,* 9 Ala. App. 449; 63 So. 693.

Action under Act and another under common law may be joined.

> *Bouchard* v *Central Vermont R. R.,* 89 A. 475.

"The proper procedure is to plead the facts, and a recovery may then be had accordingly, as the evidence may develop a case under one law or the other."

> *Vandalia R. R.* v *Stringer,* Ind. 106 N. E. 865.
>
> *Missouri &c Ry.* v *Wulf,* 226 U. S. 570.
>
> *Ullrich* v *New York &c R. R.,* 193 Fed. 768.
>
> *Jones* v *Chesapeake &c R. R.,* 149 Ky. 566; 149 S. W. 951.
>
> *St. Louis &c Ry.* v *Seale,* 229 U. S. 156; 33 S. C. 651; 57 L. Ed. 1129; Ann. Cas. 1914, c. 156.
>
> *Wabash Ry. Co.* v *Hayes,* 234 U. S. 86; 34 S. C. 729; 58 L. Ed. 1226.
>
> *Southern Ry.* v *Howerton,* 105 N. E. 1025.
>
> *Southern Ry.* v *Ansley,* 8 Ga. App. 325; 68 S. E. 1086.

"Facts which give the right to recover under the state law, and those which give the right to recover under the federal statute, constitute separate and distinct causes of action, for the federal statute is exclusive where the incident is embraced within interstate commerce service and does not apply where it is in intra-state service. The two causes of action may, however, be joined in the same complaint."

> *Midland Valley Ry.* v *Ennis,* 159 S. W. 214.

"We have no doubt that a plaintiff may join, in distinct counts, in one complaint, a sufficiently stated cause of action, arising out of the one transaction, for breach of duty under the state Employers' Liability Act and for breach of duty under the federal Employers' Liability Act; but he cannot recover as upon authority of the local statute in a case governed exclusively by the national statute, nor can he recover as upon the authority of the national statute, in a case that does not fall within the national enactment."

Ex parte Atlantic Coast Line Ry., Ala. 1914, 67 So. Rep. 256.

A common law action and another under Act may be consolidated or tried together.

Linkham v Boston &c R. R., 77 N. H. 111; 88 A. 709.

Joinder of actions under Act, state statutes and common law may be made.

> *Wabash R. R.* v *Hayes,* 234 U. S. 86; 34 Sup. Ct. 729.
>
> *Delaware &c Ry.* v *Yunkonis,* 220 F. 429; Aff. 213 F. 537.
>
> *Thomas* v *Chicago &c Ry.,* 202 F. 766.
>
> *Ullrich* v *New York &c Ry.,* 193 F. 768.
>
> *Bankson* v *Illinois Central R. R.,* 196 F. 171.
>
> *Taylor* v *Southern Ry.,* 101 N. E. 506.
>
> *Bouchard* v *Central Vermont Ry.,* 87 Vt. 399; 89 Atl. 475.

When two causes of action result in one injury, there is no misjoinder.

> *Alabama &c Ry.* v *Neal,* 8 Ala. App. 591; 62 So. 554.

Action held not dismissed by pendency of prior action.

> *Tinkham* v *Boston &c Ry.,* 77 N. H. 111; 88 Atl. 709.

Previous action, under state law, which has been dismissed, no bar.

> *Hogan* v *New York &c Ry.,* 223 F. 890.

The argument that case is governed by Act and not by state law may first be made on motion for new trial.

> *Moliter* v *Wabash R. R.,* 180 Mo. App. 84; 168 S. W. 250.

When proof shows cause of action under Act and case is brought under state law, demurrer to evidence is sufficient to raise objection.

> *Moliter* v *Wabash R. R.,* 180 Mo. App. 84; 168 S. W. 250.

Objection that Federal Act applies is in time if made when fact disclosed by proof.

> *Kamboris* v *Oregon &c Co.,* 145 Pac. 1097.

ACTION TRANSITORY, not local.

> *Anderson* v *Louisville &c R. R.,* 210 F. 689.

Pleading—Requirements.

Act need not be expressly pleaded.

"To say that the Act may not be applied to a situation which is within its provision unless in express terms the provisions of the Act be formally invoked, aside from its manifest unsoundness, considered as an original proposition, the contention is not open as it was expressly foreclosed in *Seaboard Air Line* v *Duvall*, 225 U. S. 477, 482."

Grand Trunk Ry. v *Lindsay*, 233 U. S. 42; Aff. 201 F. 836.

"The court was presumed to be cognizant of the enactment of the Employers' Liability Act and to know that with respect to the responsibility of interstate carriers by railroads to their employes injured in such commerce after its enactment it had the effect of superseding state laws upon the subject. Therefore, the pleader was not required to refer to the Federal Act and the reference actually made to the Kansas statute no more vitiated the pleading than a reference to any other repealed statute would have done."

Missouri &c Ry. v *Wulf*, 226 U. S. 570; 33 S. C. 135; 57 L. Ed. 355.

"It is not necessary to plead the terms and provisions of the Federal Act. It is only necessary to plead facts that show that the Federal Act, and not the state law, applies. This tenders an issue of fact, which, if denied by the reply, must be determined as any other issue of fact in the case. If the defendant below should fail to plead facts that would take the transaction out of the law of the forum and bring it within the operation of the federal law, then it could not be permitted over the objection of plaintiff to introduce any evidence in proof of such facts because no such issue is presented by the pleadings. If, however, the defendant does not plead facts that, if proven, would bring the transaction within the operation of the Federal law, yet if the evidence introduced by plaintiff in support of the allegations of his petition shows that he was engaged in interstate commerce, or if the defendant, without objection on the part of the plaintiff, introduced evidence of such facts, then it is the duty of the court to charge the provisions of the Federal Act, instead of the provisions of the state statutes, unless there should be a conflict of evidence, in which event an amendment should be permitted and the issue of fact submitted to the jury, with proper instructions to apply the state or the Federal law as the jury may determine the fact to be."

Erie R. R. v *Welsh*, Ohio 1913, 105 N. E. 189.

Declaration or complaint must allege facts bringing case within Act.

"When the evidence was adduced it developed that the real case was not controlled by the state statute but by the Federal statute. In short, the case pleaded was not proved and the case proved was not pleaded. In that situation, the defendant interposed the objection, grounded on the Federal statute, that the plaintiffs were not entitled to recover on the case proved. We think the objection was interposed in due time and that the state courts erred in overruling it."

St. Louis &c Ry. v *Seale,* 229 U. S. 156.

"While state as well as Federal courts are presumed to be cognizant of the Employers' Liability Act, and to recognize that such law is supreme with respect to the responsibilities of railroads engaged in interstate commerce to their employes injured or killed in such commerce, yet, before a state court is called upon to administer the Federal law in any case, the party desiring to avail himself of any right, privilege or immunity thereunder, must by appropriate pleading, or by evidence, bring to the attention of the court the fact that his cause of action or his defense falls within its terms. Obviously, it supersedes all state laws and regulations as to causes of action falling within its terms, yet in an action where neither the pleadings nor the evidence bring the cause within the purview of that Act, and the trial in the court below proceeded upon the theory that the state statute governed, this court is precluded from holding that the Federal statute should have controlled; for, necessarily, in such case the state law alone could be applied."

Chicago &c Ry. v *McBee,* Okla., 145 Pac. 331.

Plaintiff alleged that "at the time of the injury decedent was in the service of defendant as brakeman upon its said train, which was then being used and operated on one of its highways of interstate commerce, and that said cars and trains were then being used in interstate commerce, or were being used in intra-state commerce, and that one of the two states of facts is true and she does not know and cannot state which is true." The court say:

"The precise question was before this court in the case of *South Covington &c Ry.* v *Finan's Admr.*, 153 Ky. 340; 155 S. W. 742. In the first paragraph plaintiff based her right of recovery on the common law. In the second paragraph she pleaded that the defendant was engaged in interstate commerce and her decedent was injured while employed in interstate commerce, thus invoking the aid of the Federal Employers' Liability Act. In her third paragraph she rested her case on the statue of the state of Ohio. * * While the precise question has not been passed upon by the Supreme Court of the United States, its rulings on other questions of a similar character tend, we think, to sustain the views herein announced. The decisions of that court make it reasonably plain that there can be no such thing as an alternative right of action under the Federal or state law; for both cannot occupy the same field, and if the Federal statute is applicable the state law is excluded by reason of the supremacy of the former under our National Constitution. Thus in the case of *St. Louis &c Ry.* v *Seale*, 222 U. S. 156; 33 S. Ct. 651; 57 L. Ed. 1129, plaintiff's petition stated a case under the state law. It developed from the evidence that the real case was controlled, not by the state statute, but by the Federal statute. It was held that the case proved was not pleaded, and that plaintiff was not entitled to recover. In the case of *St. Louis &c Ry.* v *Hesterly*, 228 U. S. 702, 33 S. Ct. 703, 57 L. Ed. 1031, it was held that defendant was not estopped to rely on the Federal statute by a plea of contributory negligence on the ground that the right of action was in the plaintiff, and as he relied on the state law, defendant had no choice if it was to defend on facts. In the case at bar the motion to elect was made in due time. Defendant had the right to know in advance under which law it would be required to defend."

Louisville &c Ry. v *Strange's Admr.*, Ky., 161 S. W. Rep. 239.

DECLARATION OR COMPLAINT must allege facts showing that defendant was a common carrier engaged in interstate commerce and that plaintiff was in its employment and in the performance of his duty in connection with such interstate commerce traffic at time of injury.

> *Walton* v *Southern Ry.*, 179 Fed. 175.
> *St. Louis R. R.* v *Hesterly*, 98 Ark. 240; 135 S. W. 874.

Complaint may state cause of action under Act, Safety Act and state statute.

> *Hayes* v *Wabash R. R.*, 234 U. S. 86; 180 Ill. App. 511.

Where Act is not pleaded by either party, dismissal held error.

> *Bitondo* v *New York Central Ry.*, 149 N. Y. S. 339; 163 App. Div. 823.

Act controls, when complaint states facts, bringing cause within the same, although a cause of action is also stated under state law.

> *Peck* v *Boston &c R. R.*, 223 F. 448.

Plaintiff must show that case is within Act.

> *Chicago &c Ry.* v *McBee*, Okla., 145 Pac. 331.

Complaint held properly drawn.

> *Delaware &c Ry.* v *Yurkonis*, 220 F. 429; Aff. 213 F. 537; App. Dis. 238 U. S. 439; 35 S. Ct. 902.
> *McIntosh* v *St. Louis &c Ry.*, 182 Mo. App. 288; 168 S. W. 821.

Separate counts may declare on Act and state law, but recovery can be had on only one charge.

> *Ex Parte Atlantic Coast Line Ry.*, 67 So. Rep. 256; Rev. 9 Ala. App. 499; 63 So. 693.
> *Atkinson* v *Bullard, Ga.*, 80 S. E. Rep. 220.

Complaint may be amended to state cause of action under state law.

> *Midland Valley R. R.* v *Ennis*, 159 S. W. 214.

Omission to allege facts regarding interstate commerce may be supplied by answer.

Vickery v *New London &c Ry.*, 87 Conn. 634; 89 A. 277.

White v *Central Vermont Ry.*, 89 Atl. 618.

When declaration alleges common law action and replication counts on Act, there is departure.

Niles v *Central Vermont Ry.*, 89 Atl. Rep. 629.

Where petition does not refer to Act or state statute, motion to specify character of business should be made.

McIntosh v *St. Louis &c Ry.*, 182 Mo. App. 288; 168 S. W. 821.

Complaint held good.

Pittsburgh &c Ry. v *Farmers &c Co.*, 108 N. E. Rep. 108.

Allegations are necessary, showing both parties to have been engaged in interstate commerce.

> *St. Louis &c Ry.* v *Hesterly,* 98 Ark. 240; 135 S. W. 874.
>
> *Ismura* v *Great Northern Ry.,* 58 Wash. 316; 108 Pac. 774.
>
> *Bay* v *Merrill & Ring Lumber Co.,* 211 Fed. 717.
>
> *Allen* v *Tuscarora &c Ry.,* 229 Pa. 97; 78 Atl. 34; 30 L. R. A. (N. S.) 1096.

Complaint must allege that plaintiff was engaged in the performance of his duties or work within scope of his employment.

> 189 Ill. App. 89.

Complaint need not be in terms drawn under Act.

> *Southern Ry.* v *Howerton,* 101 N. E. 121.

Formal reference to Act not necessary.

> *Denoyer* v *Railway Transfer Co.,* 149 N. W. 175.
>
> *Southern Ry.* v *Ansley,* 68 S. E. Rep. 1086.

General allegation of negligence, sufficient under state law, is good.

> *Louisville &c Ry.* v *Stewart's Admx.,* 156 Ky. 550; 161 S. W. 557; Mod. 163 S. W. 755.

Averments of due care in count under Safety Act, surplusage.

> *Lucas* v *Peoria &c Ry.,* 171 Ill. App. 1.

Petition held sufficient.

> *Kelly's Admx.* v *Chesapeake &c Ry.,* 201 Fed. 602.
>
> *Ahrens* v *Chicago &c Ry.,* 141 N. W. Rep. 297.
>
> *Illinois Central Ry.* v *Stewart,* 223 Fed. 30.

Complaint held insufficient.

> *Vickery* v *New London &c Co.,* 87 Conn. 634; 89 Atl. 277.

PLEA of engagement in interstate commerce, held sufficient.

> *San Antonio &c Ry.* v *Wagner,* 166 S. W. Rep. 24.

In action under state law, Act must be pleaded as defence.

> *St. Louis &c Ry.* v *Seale,* 148 N. W. 1099.

Plea of contributory negligence which fails to allege knowledge of plaintiff of danger or that danger was apparent to ordinary observation, defective.

> *Illinois Central Ry.* v *Lowery,* 63 So. Rep. 952; 49 L. R. A. 1149.

Plea held sufficient, although not alleging knowledge of defect or failure in due care to acquire knowledge.

> *Atlantic Coast Line Ry.* v *Jones,* 9 Ala. App. 499; 63 So. Rep. 693.

Plea, assumption of risk, see

> *Wabash Ry.* v *Gretzinger,* 104 N. E. Rep. 69.
> *Vickery* v *New London Ry.,* 87 Conn. 634; 89 Atl. Rep. 277.

Procedure—Requirements.

RULES OF STATE LAW as to pleading, evidence and procedure should be conformed to, except as modified by Act.

> *McAdow* v *Kansas &c Ry.*, 164 S. W. 185.
> *Fleming* v *Norfolk &c Ry.*, 76 S. E. Rep. 212.
> *Louisville &c Ry.* v *Johnson's Admx.*, 161 Ky. 824; 171 S. W. 847.
> *Central Vermont Ry.* v *White*, 238 U. S. 508.

Federal practice need not be followed.

> *Howell* v *Atlantic Coast Line Ry.*, 99 S. Car. 417; 83 S. E. 639.

State court is not bound to follow Federal practice by directing verdict upon preponderance of evidence.

> *Louisville &c Ry.* v *Holloway's Admr.*, 163 Ky. 125; 173 S. W. 343.

VERDICT may be returned by three-fourths of jury (under state law).

> *Chesapeake &c Ry.* v *Kelly's Admr.,* 161 Ky. 655; 171 S. W. 185; Reh. den. 160 Ky. 296; 168 S. W. 736.
>
> *Louisville &c Ry.* v *Winkler,* 162 Ky. 843; 173 S. W. 151.

Five-sixth jury law applies.

> *Winters* v *Minneapolis &c Ry.,* 126 Minn. 260; 148 N. W. 106-1096.
>
> *Bambolis* v *Minneapolis &c Ry.,* 128 Minn. 112; 150 N. W. 85.

Interest on verdict not allowed.

> *Norton* v *Erie R. R.,* 148 N. Y. S. 771; Aff. 144 N. Y. 656.

Where rules of law, governing the trial, are the same in Federal and state procedure, it is immaterial whether action and judgment proceed under Federal or state law.

> *Illinois Central R. R.* v *Nelson,* 212 F. 69.

EVIDENCE must establish that defendant owned and operated railroad as common carrier engaged in interstate or foreign commerce, and that plaintiff was injured while employed by defendant in such commerce and in course of his duties.

> *Bay* v *Merrill & Ring L. Co.*, 211 F. 717.

Evidence which would bring case to jury under state law will do so under Act.

> *Louisville &c Ry.* v *Winkler*, 162 Ky. 843; 173 S. W. 151.

Negligence of carrier must be shown.

> *Cincinnati &c Ry.* v *Goldston*, 156 Ky. 410; 161 S. W. 246.

Rule of evidence as to negligence, *res ipsa loquitur*, not applicable.

> *Curtis* v *New York &c Ry.*, 144 N. Y. S. 1007; 159 App. Div. 757.

INSTRUCTION in language of section held proper.

> *Devine* v *Chicago &c Ry.*, 185 Ill. App. 488; Aff.
> 226 Ill. 248; 107 N. E. 595.

Court should instruct whether action comes within Act or under common law rules.

> *Hoag* v *Washington &c Ry.*, 144 Pac. 574; Mod.
> 147 Pac. 756.

Where cause based on both Act and state statute and case shown to be within Act, affirmative charge should be given on state statute count.

> *Ex Parte Coast Line Ry.*, 67 So. Rep. 256; Rev.
> 9 Ala. 499; 63 So. 693.

Where neither party relies on Section 4, failure to charge in regard thereto, not error.

> *Devine* v *Chicago &c Ry.*, 266 Ill. 248; 107 N. E.
> 595; Aff. 185 Ill. App. 488.

Instruction as to negligence, violent jerking, see:

> *Cincinnati &c Ry.* v *Goldston*, 156 Ky. 410; 161
> S. W. 246.

"Where an instruction embodies several propositions of law, to some of which no objection could properly be taken, a general exception to the entire instruction will not entitle the exceptor to take advantage of a mistake or error in some single or minor proposition therein."

> *Norfolk* v *Western Ry.*, 229 U. S. 114.

Appeal and Error—Requirements.

THE SUPREME COURT OF THE UNITED STATES will consider only questions of interpretation of the Act and not those involving considerations of general law, depending in no sense upon the particular significance of the Act, unless it clearly appears that error has been committed.

> *Southern Ry.* v *Gadd*, 233 U. S. 572.

"A Federal right, in order to be reviewable here, must be set up and denied in a state court, and such claim of denial is not properly brought to the attention of this court when it appears that the state court declined to pass on the question because it was not raised in the trial court, as required by state practice."

> *Louisville &c Ry.* v *Woodford*. 234 U. S. 46; 34 S. Ct. 739; 58 L. E. 1202.

The Supreme Court of United States will confirm a judgment of the Circuit Court of Appeals, where a question of interpretation of Act is not involved.

> *Southern Ry.* v *Gadd*, 233 U. S. 572; 34 Sup. Ct. 696; Aff. 207 F. 277; 125 C. C. A. 21.

Allegation that plaintiff was engaged in mining coal for interstate commerce does not necessarily bring case within Act for review by U. S. Supreme Court.

> *Delaware &c Ry.* v *Yurkonis*, 238 U. S. 439; 35 Sup. Ct. 902; Des. App. 220 F. 429; Aff. 213 F. 537.

Decree of state court, refusing recovery because of contributory negligence, is not controlling.

> *Cincinnati &c Ry.* v *Swamis' Admr.*, 160 Ky. 458; 169 S. W. 886.

"The point that the Indiana statute had been superseded by this Act, not having been specially set up in the state court and there passed upon, it is obvious that the point has not been saved."

> *Chicago &c Ry.* v *Hackett*, 228 U. S. 559; 33 Sup. Ct. 581; 57 L. Ed. 966.

> See *Chicago &c Ry.* v *Holliday*, 145 Pac. 786.

Where claim to immunity from state legislation is shown by record, the question of the Federal right will be considered by the United States Supreme Court.

North Carolina R. R. v *Zachary,* 232 U. S. 248.

The Supreme Court of United States will not consider questions of matters of pleading, admission of evidence or of general law, where construction of Act is not involved.

Central Vermont Ry. v *White,* 35 Sup. Ct. 865; Aff. 87 Vt. 330; 89 Atl. 616.

Yazoo v *Midland &c Ry.,* 235 U. S. 376; 35 S. Ct. 130; Aff. 125 C. C. A. 25; 207 F. 281.

Misleading instructions may serve as basis for writ of error to Supreme Court.

Seaboard Air Line v *Padgett,* 236 U. S. 668; 35 Sup. Ct. 481; Aff. 99 S. C. 356; 83 S. E. 633.

A decision that deceased was an employee of an express company, and that the liability of the railroad was not controlled by the Act, is not reviewable in the U. S. Supreme Court.

Missouri &c Ry. v *West,* 232 U. S. 682; 34 S. Ct. 471; Dis. *Holmes* v *Jewell,* 134 P. 655.

Amendment of 1910 withdraws right of removal and requires review of Federal questions by writ of error to state court.

Lloyd v *North Carolina R. R.,* 162 N. C. 485; 78 S. E. 489.

A judgment of non-suit on ground of failure to prove employment in interstate commerce does not present a question of jurisdiction to sustain direct writ of error to Supreme Court.

Farrugin v *Phila. &c Ry.,* 233 U. S. 352; 34 S. C. 591.

Limitation—Two years.

Limitation of two years controls state law.

> *Shannon* v *Boston &c Ry.*, 77 N. H. 349; 92 Atl. 167.

AMENDMENT after two years so as to bring case within Act, held not introducing new cause of action.

> *Smith* v *Atlantic Coast Line Ry.*, 210 Fed. 761.

An amendment, substituting plaintiff as personal representative of deceased for herself as sole beneficiary, is not equivalent to commencing a new action, barred after two years, even though the original declaration is based on a state statute.

> *Missouri &c Ry.* v *Wulf*, 226 U. S. 570.

"The change was in form rather than in substance. It introduced no new or different cause of action, nor did it set up any different state of facts as the ground of action, and therefore it relates back to the beginning of the suit." *Ib.*

Exemption—Contracts for—void.

"If Congress possesses the power to impose the liability, which we here hold that it does, it also possesses the power to insure its efficacy by prohibiting any contract, rule, regulation or device in evasion of it."

Phila. &c R. R. v *Schubert*, 224 U. S. 603.

Second Employers' Liability Cases, 223 U. S. 1.

"That the provisions of § 5 were intended to apply as well to existing as to future contracts and regulations of the described character, cannot be doubted. * * * Prior arrangements were necessarily subject to this paramount authority. The power of Congress, in its regulation of interstate commerce, to impose this liability, was not fettered by the necessity of maintaining existing arrangements and stipulations which would conflict with the execution of its policy."

Phila., Balt., & Wash. R. R. v *Schubert*, 224 U. S. 603.

Contract with express messenger, held void.

Taylor v *Wells Fargo & Co.*, 220 F. 796.

Acceptance of relief or benefits does not bar action.

Wagner v *Chicago & A. R. R.*, 265 Ill. 245; 106 N. E. 809; Aff. 180 Ill. App. 196.

Exemption agreement by which employe must present written claim within thirty days after accident, void.

Chicago &c R. R. v *Pearce*, Ark., 175 S. W. 1160.

Benefits paid by lessee railroad may be set off.

Wagner v *Chicago &c R. R.*, 180 Ill. App. 196; Aff. 265 Ill. 245; 106 N. E. 809.

Existing and future contracts of relief are condemned.

Philadelphia &c R. R. v *Schubert*, 224 U. S. 603; 32 S. C. 589; 56 L. Ed. 91; Aff. 36 App. Div. 565.

Action for Death—Representative must bring—
PERSONAL REPRESENTATIVE alone may sue; plaintiff must be administrator or executor, not widow nor relative, in own name.

> *Fithian* v *St. Louis &c Ry.*, 188 F. 842.
> *La Casse* v *New Orleans &c Ry.*, 64 So. 1162.
> *St. Louis &c Ry.* v *Brothers*, 165 S. W. 488.
> *Penny* v *New Orleans &c Ry.*, 135 La. 962; 66 So. 313.
> *Missouri &c Ry.* v *Lenahan*, 135 Pac. 383.
> *Anderson* v *Louisville & N. Ry.*, 210 F. 689.
> *Vaughan* v *St. Louis &c Ry.*, 177 Mo. App. 155; 164 S. W. 144.
> *Rich* v *St. Louis &c Ry.*, 166 Mo. App. 379; 148 S. W. 1011.
> *Cincinnati &c Ry.* v *Bonham*, 130 Tenn. 435; 171 S. W. 79.
> *Missouri &c Ry.* v *Wulf*, 226 U. S. 570.
> *American R. R.* v *Birch*, 224 U. S. 547.

Personal representative means executor or administrator.

> *Rivera* v *Atchison &c Ry.*, 149 S. W. 223.

Anciliary as well as domicilary administrator may sue.

> *Anderson* v *Louisville &c Ry.*, 210 F. 689.

Appearance as administratrix, after widow has obtained judgment, does not cure error.

> *Dungan* v *St. Louis &c Ry.*, 165 S. W. 1116.

Widow cannot recover for herself and as next friend for children.

> *Kansas City &c Ry.* v *Pope*, 152 S. W. 185; Reh. den. 153 S. W. 763.

"If the Federal statute was applicable, the right of recovery, if any, was in the personal representative of the deceased, and no one else could maintain the action."

St. Louis &c Ry. v *Seale*, 229 U. S. 156, 158.

Troxell v *Delaware &c R. R.*, 227 U. S. 434.

Missouri &c Ry. v *Wulf*, 226 U. S. 570.

"The words of the Act are too clear to be other than strictly followed. They give an action for damages to the person injured or, 'in case of his death * * * to his or her personal representative.' It is true that the recovery of the damages is not for the benefit of the estate of the deceased but for the benefit 'of the surviving widow or husband and children.' But this distinction between the parties to sue and the parties to be benefited by the suit, makes clear the purpose of Congress. To this purpose we must yield. * * * The act gives the right of action to personal representatives only."

American R. R. v *Birch*, 224 U. S. 547.

Eastern Ry. v *Ellis*, Texas, 1913, 153 S. W. 701.

Plaintiff cannot intervene in representative capacity on appeal, but case will be remanded.

Missouri &c Ry. v *Lenahan*, 135 Pac. 383.

That right of action is in representative and not widow, may be urged on appeal.

LaCassa v *New Orleans &c Ry.*, 64 So. 1012.

Where instruction has been refused, that representative must sue, and new trial asked on such ground, question is presented for appeal.

Cincinnati &c Ry. v *Bonham*, 130 Tenn. 435; 171 S. W. 79.

Action for Death—Act grants new cause of—

Act grants new cause of action for wrongful death, independent of rights of deceased.

> *Thomas* v *Chicago & N. W. Ry.*, 202 F. 766.
> *Fogarty* v *North Pac. Ry.*, 147 Pac. 652.
> *Kansas City Southern Ry.* v *Brownwood*, 166 S. W. 83.

Right of action is distinct cause of action, not survival of decedent's.

> *Farley* v *New York, N. H. &c Ry.*, 87 Conn. 328; 87 A. 990.

Right of action of employe is extinguished by death.

> *Garrett* v *Louisville &c Ry.*, 235 U. S. 308; 35 S. C. 32; Aff. 117 C. C. A. 109; 197 F. 715.

Decedent's right of action does not survive.

> *Cain* v *Southern Ry.*, 199 F. 211.

Decedent's right of action for suffering does not survive before amendments.

> *Garrett* v *Louisville &c Ry.*, 197 F. 715; 117 C. C. A. 109.

Right of action must be based entirely on Act.

> *Missouri &c Ry.* v *Lenahan*, 135 Pac. 383.

Did not exist at common law.

> *Fithian* v *St. Louis &c Ry.*, 188 F. 842.

Damages which deceased might have recovered are not included. (Previous to amendment.)

> *Thomas* v *Chicago & N. W. Ry.*, 202 F. 766.

Only right of action is for benefit of next of kin.

> *St. Louis &c Ry.* v *Hesterly,* 288 U. S. 702; 33 S. C. 703; 57 L. Ed. 1031; Rev. 98 Ark. 240; 135 S. W. 874.

Where employe survives accident for several hours, action lies by representative.

> *Michigan Central R. R.* v *Vreeland,* 227 U. S. 59; 33 S. C. 192; Rev. 189 F. 495.

Action by representative is not limited to cases of instantaneous death.

> *Michigan Central R. R.* v *Vreeland,* 227 U. S. 59.

Where decedent survives an appreciable length of time, breathing ten minutes, action survives.

> *Capital Trust Co.* v *Great Northern Ry.,* 149 N. W. 14.

Prior judgment of widow for benefit of herself and children bars suit under Act.

> *Delaware &c R. R.* v *Troxell,* 200 F. 44; 118 C. C. A. 272; Aff. 227 U. S. 434; 33 S. C. 274.

Letters of administration may issue, although the deceased left no other property.

> *Gulf &c Ry.* v *Beezley,* 153 S. W. 651.

Inchoate right is sufficient.

> *Eastern Ry.* v *Ellis,* 153 S. W. 701.

Action for Death—Beneficiaries.

Act supersedes all state statutes upon the subject covered by it, and distribution of amount recovered is determined by Act and not by state law. Where a widow sues as administrator, parents have no claim.

Taylor v *Taylor*, 232 U. S. 363.

Act gives no right to relatives not dependent.

Jones v *Charleston &c Ry.*, 98 S. C. 197; 82 S. E. 415.

Reasonable expectation of benefit to father held sufficient, and no proof required that deceased would have contributed to his support.

Raines v *Southern Ry.*, 85 S. E. 294.

Reasonable expectation of pecuniary benefit is sufficient, without showing actual dependency.

Dooley v *Seaboard Air Line Ry.*, 163 N. C. 454; 79 S. E. 970.

Moffett v *Baltimore &c Ry.*, 220 F. 39; 135 C. C. A. 607.

Reasonable expectation of pecuniary benefit is for jury.

Moffett v *Baltimore &c O. Ry.*, 220 F. 39; 135 C. C. A. 607.

Married sister, who had boarded deceased and to whom he had made monthly contributions of money, held not dependent nor entitled to recover.

Southern Ry. v *Vessel*, 68 So. 336.

Act is remedial and construed liberally in favor of beneficiaries.

McFarland v *Oregon &c Ry.*, 138 Pac. 458.

Question who are next of kin is determined by state law.

Kenney v *Seaboard Air Line Ry.*, 82 S. E. 968.

Act confers benefit only for relatives specified.

Thomas v *Chicago & N. W. Ry.*, 202 F. 766.

Act does not abrogate right of action of parent, guardian or representative for death under Oregon statute, repealing only what conflicts.

McFarland v *Oregon Electric Ry.*, 138 Pac. 458.

Each class specified excludes succeeding classes. Mother has no right to recover where decedent leaves widow and child.

St. Louis &c Ry. v *Geer*, 149 S. W. 1178.

Minor son by decedent's divorced wife, held to have reasonable expectation of pecuniary benefit.

McGarvey's Guardian v *McGarvey's Adm.*, 163 Ky. 242; 173 S. W. 765.

Child, not dependent on decedent and having no reasonable expectation of pecuniary benefit from him, cannot participate in recovery.

McGarvey's Guardian v *McGarvey's Adm.*, 163 Ky. 242; 175 S. W. 765.

Sister of decedent, who had contributed to her support, held entitled to recover.

Richelieu v *Union Pac. Ry.*, 97 Neb. 360; 149 N. W. 772.

Wife, temporarily separated from decedent at time of his death, may recover.

Dunbar v *Charleston &c Ry.*, 186 F. 175.

Abandonment by husband of wife and minor child is material only in mitigation of damages.

Fogarty v *Northern Pac. Ry.*, 147 Pac. 652.

Brother, dependent: See *Jones* v *Charleston &c Ry.*, 98 S. C. 197; 82 S. E. 415.

WIDOW is not required to elect whether to rely on one suit under Act or one in her own name under state law.

> *Corbett* v *Boston & M. R. R.*, 219 Mass. 351; 107 N. E. 60.

Widow need not elect between her cause of action for the benefit of the estate and that for herself and next of kin.

> *St. Louis &c Ry.* v *Rodgers*, 176 S. W. 696.

"If the action included a right under § 9, the recovery was for her benefit exclusively, as the widow of the decedent. The language of the section is that the right of action given to the employe survives to his personal representatives for the benefits of his parents only when there is no widow."

> *Taylor* v *Taylor*, 232 U. S. 363.

"Two of the plaintiffs, the father and mother, in whose favor there was a separate recovery, are not even beneficiaries under the Federal statute, there being a surviving widow; and she was not entitled to recover in her own name, but only through the deceased's personal representative."

> *St. Louis &c Ry.* v *Seale*, 229 U. S. 156.

An unmarried, illegitimate son has no next of kin.

> *Wilson's Admr.*, 157 Ky. 460; 163 S. W. 493.

ALIENS: Act gives right of recovery for benefit of non-resident aliens.

"The policy of the Act accords with and finds expression in the universality of its language. Its purpose is to give something more than to give compensation for the negligence of railroad companies. It is for the protection of life that compensation for its destruction is given and to those who have relation to it. What difference can it make where they reside? It is the fact of their relation to the life destroyed that is the circumstance to be considered, whether we consider the injury received by them or the influence of that relation upon the life destroyed."

McGovern v *Philadelphia &c R. R.*, 235 U. S. 389; 35 S. C. 127; Rev. 109 F. 975; 213 F. 647; 234 U. S. 86; Rev. 180 Ill. App. 511.

Bambolis v *Minneapolis &c Ry.*, 128 Minn. 112; 150 N. W. 385.

Act permits suit for death of non-citizen employe, killed in another state.

Waring v *Baltimore & O. Ry.*, 33 Oh. Cir. Ct. R. 194.

Action for Death—Pecuniary loss—

"Recent opinions of this court have laid down the rule concerning the measure of pecuniary damages to beneficiaries which may be recovered under this Act. A recovery, therefor, by the administrator, is in trust for designated individuals and must be based upon their actual pecuniary loss."

Kansas City Southern Ry. v *Leslie,* 238 U. S. 599.

Michigan Central R. R. v *Vreeland,* 227 U. S. 59.

American R. R. v *Didricksen,* 227 U. S. 145.

Gulf, Colorado &c Ry. v *McGinnis,* 228 U. S. 173.

North Carolina R. R. v *Zachary,* 232 U. S. 248.

Norfolk & Western Ry. v *Holbrook,* 235 U. S. 625.

"In every instance the award must be based upon money values, the amount of which can be ascertained only upon a view of the peculiar facts presented. In the present case there was testimony concerning the personal qualities of the deceased and the interest which he took in his family. It was proper, therefore, to charge that the jury might take into consideration the care, attention, instruction, training, advice and guidance which the evidence showed he reasonably might have been expected to give his children during their minority, and to include the pecuniary value thereof in the damages assessed. But there was nothing—indeed there could be nothing—to show the hypothetic injury which might have befallen some unidentified adult beneficiary or dependent next of kin. The ascertained circumstances must govern in every case. We think the trial court plainly erred when it declared that where the persons suffering the injury are the dependent widow and infant children of a deceased husband and father the pecuniary injury suffered would be much greater than where the beneficiaries were adults or dependents who were mere next of kin."

Norfolk &c Western Ry. v *Holbrook,* 235 U. S. 625; Rev. 215 F. 687. (Three judges dissenting.)

"The statutory action of an administrator is not for the equal benefit of each of the surviving relatives for whose benefit the suit is brought. Though the judgment may be for a gross amount, the interest of each beneficiary must be measured by his or her individual pecuniary loss. That apportionment is for the jury to return. This will, of course, exclude any recovery on behalf of such as show no pecuniary loss."

Gulf &c Ry. v McGinnis, 228 U. S. 173.

"The recovery must be limited to compensating those relatives for whose benefit the administrator sues as are shown to have sustained some pecuniary loss."

Gulf &c Ry. v McGinnis, 228 U. S. 173.

Michigan Central Ry. v Vreeland, 227 U. S. 59.

American R. R. v Didricksen, 227 U. S. 145.

"The cause of action which was created on behalf of the injured employe did not survive his death nor pass to his representatives. But the Act, in case of death of such employe from his injury, creates a new and distinct right of action for the benefit of the dependent relatives named in the statute. The damages recoverable are limited to such loss as results to them because they have been deprived of a reasonabl expectation of pecuniary benefits by the wrongful death of the injured employe. The damage is limited strictly to the financial loss thus sustained. The court below went beyond the limitation by charging the jury that they might, in estimating the damages, 'take into consideration the fact that they are the father and mother of the deceased and the fact that they are deprived of his society and any care and consideration he might take of them, or have for them during his life.' The loss of the society or companionship of a son is a deprivation not to be measured by any money standard. It is not a pecuniary loss under a statute such as this. Laying out of consideration the indefiniteness of the term, 'care and consideration,' as elements in addition to the loss and damage of such pecuniary assistance as the parents of the deceased might have reasonably anticipated from their son, it is enough for the purpose of this case to say that there was no allegation of such loss, nor any evidence relating to the subject, or from which its pecuniary value might have been estimated."

American R. R. of Porto Rico v Didricksen, 227 U. S. 145.

"The pecuniary loss is not dependent upon any legal liability of the injured person to the beneficiary. That is not the sole test. There must, however, appear some reasonable expectation of pecuniary assistance or support of which they have been deprived. Compensation for such loss manifestly does not include damages by way of recompense for grief or wounded feelings, *   *   *   nor the inestimable loss of society and companionship. *   *   *   This widow may have been deprived of some actual customary service of deceased, capable of measurement by some pecuniary standard, and in some degree that service might include as elements care and advice. But there was neither allegation nor evidence of such loss of service, care or advice. The jury were erroneously told to estimate the value from their own experiences."

Mich. Cent. R. R. Co., v *Vreeland,* 227 U. S. 59.

"In the nature of the case, evidence cannot be very definite as to the actual amount of the pecuniary loss sustained in a case, but it does devolve upon plaintiff to show those general facts which are necessarily within the general knowledge of the beneficiaries and which bear upon the financial resources and prospects of themselves, as well as those of decedent."

McCullough v *Chicago &c Ry.,* 160 Iowa 524; 146 N. W. Rep. 70.

"The proper estimate can usually be arrived at with approximate accuracy by taking into account the calling of the deceased, and the income derived therefrom; his health, age, talents and habits of industry; his success in life in the past, as well as the amount of money in aid or services which he was accustomed to furnish the next of kin; and if the verdict is greatly in excess of this sum thus arrived at, the court will set it aside or cut it down."

Hutchins v *St. Paul Ry.,* 44 Minn. 5; 46 N. W. 79.

Approved *McCullough* v *Chicago &c Ry.,* 160 Iowa 524; 146 Pac. Rep. 70.

"The proper measure of damages is the present worth of the amount which it is reasonably probable the deceased would have contributed to the support of the parent during the latter's expectancy of life, in proportion to the amount he was contributing at the time of his death, not exceeding his expectancy of life, though it would seem that the rule is not to be applied with mathematical strictness, and that the jury may properly take into consideration the increasing wants of the parents and the increasing ability of the child to support them."

> *McCullough* v *Chicago &c Ry.*, 160 Iowa 524; 146 Pac. 70.
>
> *Richmond* v *Chicago &c Ry.*, 87 Mich. 374; 49 N. W. 621.
>
> *International &c Ry.* v *Kindred*, 57 Tex. 491.
>
> *Texas &c Ry.* v *Lester*, 75 Tex. 56; 12 S. W. 955.

The damages are to be based upon the pecuniary loss sustained by the beneficiary.

> *Gulf, Colorado &c Ry.* v *McGinnis*, 228 U. S. 173.
>
> *Michigan Central R. R.* v *Vreeland*, 227 U. S. 59.
>
> *North Carolina R. R.* v *Zachary*, 232 U. S. 248.
>
> *St. Louis &c Ry.* v *Conarty*, 155 S. W. 93.
>
> *Fogarty* v *Northern Pac. Ry.*, 147 Pac. 652.

Act gives compensation for actual pecuniary loss of each survivor, not for destruction of earning power.

> *Chesapeake &c Ry.* v *Dwyer's Admx.*, 163 S. W. 752.

MEASURE OF DAMAGES: Act makes the measure of damages the pecuniary loss, not the value of net earnings, based on expectancy.

> *Henney* v *Seaboard Air Line Ry.*, 165 N. C. 99;
> 80 S. E. 1078.

Measure of damages is what will compensate surviving relatives for actual pecuniary loss.

> *Louisville & N. R. R.* v *Johnson's Admx.*, 161 Ky. 824; 171 S. W. 847.

Measure of damages for children is such amount as deceased would reasonably be expected to have contributed to their support and education.

> *Kansas City &c Ry.* v *Roe*, 150 Pac. 1035.

"In some cases, the evidence has been held sufficient to sustain a finding that there was a reasonable expectation of pecuniary benefit, although the evidence fell short of showing that assistance was actually furnished."

> *McCullough* v *Chicago &c Ry.*, 160 Iowa 524; 146 Pac. Rep. 70.
> *Hopper* v *Denver &c Ry.*, 155 F. 273; 84 C. C. A. 21.

The measure of damages, as determined by the Supreme Court of the United States, should be followed.

> *St. Louis &c Ry.* v *Hesterly*, 228 U. S. 702; 33 S. C. 703; 57 L. Ed. 1031; Rev. 98 Ark. 240; 135 S. W. 874.
> *Nashville &c Ry.* v *Henry*, 158 Ky. 88; 164 S. W. 310.
> *McAdow* v *Kansas City &c Ry.*, 164 S. W. 188.
> *Cincinnati &c Ry.* v *Nolan*, 161 Ky. 205; 170 S. W. 650.

Rule of Federal courts as to measure of damages, controls those of a state court.

> *Louisville &c Ry.* v *Stewart's Admr.*, 163 S. W. 755; modifying 156 Ky. 550; 161 S. W. 557.

Reasonable expectation of mother of pecuniary benefit, evidence held sufficient for jury.

> *Moffett* v *Balt. &c R. R.*, 220 F. 39.

Measure of damages is pecuniary loss, not deprivation of comfort, society, support and protection.

> *Fisher* v *Portland Ry.*, 145 Pac. 277; Rev. 143
> Pac. 992.

Suffering and bereavement may not be considered as elements of compensation.

> *McCullough* v *Chicago, R. I. & P. R. R.*, 142 N.
> W. 67.

Value of services, prospective gifts, etc., are elements of compensation.

> *McCullough* v *Chicago, R. I. & P. R. R.*, 142 N.
> W. 67.

Loss of comfort, society and protection, not included.

> *McFarland* v *Oregon El. Ry.*, 138 Pac. 458.

Damages are limited to such amount as results from a parent being deprived of a reasonable expectancy of pecuniary benefit.

> *Dooley* v *Seaboard Air Line Ry.*, 163 N. C. 454;
> 79 S. E. 970.

Damages are limited to loss actually sustained and not by state law fixing limit of $10,000.

> *Devine* v *Chicago, R. I & P. Ry.*, 266 Ill. 248;
> 107 N. W. 595; Aff. 185 Ill. App. 488.

Amount may exceed limit of state statute.

"The Federal Act limits the right of recovery to the pecuniary damages actually sustained by the next of kin of deceased, but it does not place any arbitrary limit on the amount that may be recovered. Plainly it would seem to be the intention of the Act that recovery may be had for the full pecuniary damages actually sustained by the next of kin.

Damages are not restricted to amount yielding income equal to what dependents would have received.

> *Chesapeake &c R. R.* v *Dwyer's Admx.*, 162 Ry.
> 427; 172 S. W. 18.

Measure of damages considered.

> *Chesapeake & O. Ry.* v *Kelly's Admx.*, 160 Ky.
> 296; 169 S. W. 736; Reh. den. 161 Ky. 655;
> 171 S. W. 185.
> *Kansas City T. R.* v *Leslie*, 167 S. W. 83.

EXPENSES of medical attendance, a reasonable sum for pain and suffering and a fair recompense for what plaintiff would otherwise have earned, allowable.

> *Nashville &c Ry.* v *Henry,* 158 Ky. 88; 164 S. W. 310.

Burial expenses and funeral charges are not included.

> *Collins* v *Penna. R. R.,* 148 N. Y. S. 777; 163 App. Div. 452.

Damages for decedent's pain and suffering not recoverable, where death is instantaneous.

> *Moffett* v *Baltimore & O. R. R.,* 220 F. 39; 155 C. C. A. 607.

INSTRUCTION to consider as elements of damages, care, instruction and training by one of deceased's disposition, which might have been expected by his wife and children, held proper.

> *St. Louis &c Ry.* v *Rodgers,* 176 S. W. 696.

Instruction to consider age, health, occupation and earning capacity of deceased and allow such amount, less personal expenses, error.

> *Kansas City S. Ry.* v *Leslie,* 35 S. C. 844; 59 L. Ed. —; Rev. 167 S. W. 83; 112 Ark. 305.

LIFE INSURANCE; evidence of collecting, held harmless error.

> *Brabham* v *Baltimore &c R. R..* 220 F. 35.

Action for Death—Damages for decedent's pain—

"Such pain and suffering as are substantially contemporaneous with death or mere incidents to it, as also the short periods of insensibility which sometimes intervene between fatal injuries and death, afford no basis for a separate estimation or award of damages under this statute. By the common law the death of a human being, although wrongfully caused, affords no basis for a recovery of damages, and a right of action for personal injuries dies with the person injured. Therefore, in cases like this, the right of recovery depends entirely upon statute law. Here the statute is not applicable because superseded by this Act. * * * This cause of action is independent of any cause of action which the decedent had, and includes no damages which he might have recovered for his injury if he had survived. It is one beyond that which the deceased had— one proceeding upon altogether different principles. It is a liability for the loss and damage sustained by relatives dependent upon the decedent.

"It is, therefore, a liability for the pecuniary damage to them and for that only. The cause of action which was created in behalf of the injured employe did not survive his death, nor pass to his representative. But the act, in case of the death of such an employe from his injury, creates a new and distinct right of action for the benefit of the dependent relatives named in the statute. The damages recoverable are limited to such loss as results to them because they have been deprived of a reasonable expectation of pecuniary benefits by the wrongful death of the injured employe. The damage is limited strictly to the financial loss thus sustained. * * * Without abrogating or curtailing either of the two distinct rights of action under the original Act, the new Section 9 in the Amendment of April 5, 1910, provides in exact words that the right given to the injured person 'shall survive' to his personal representative 'for the benefit of' the same relatives in whose behalf the other right is given. * * * This provision means that the right existing in the injured person at his death—a right covering his loss and suffering while he lived but taking no account of his premature death or of what he would have earned or accomplished in the natural span of life—shall survive to his personal representative to the end that it may be enforced and the proceeds paid to the relatives indicated. And when this provision and § 1 are read together the conclusion is unavoidable that the personal representative is to recover on behalf of the designated beneficiaries, not only such damages as will compensate them for their own pecuniary loss, but also such damages as will be reasonably compensatory for the loss and suffering of the injured person while he lived. * * * One claim begins where the other ends, and a recovery of both in the same action is not a double recovery for a single wrong but a single recovery for a double wrong.

* * * This award of $5,000 damages for pain and suffering, even though extreme, for so short a period as approximately thirty minutes, does seem large, but the power, and with it the duty and responsibility of dealing with this matter rested upon the court below. It involves only a question of fact and is not open to reconsideration here. Judgment affirmed."

> *St. Louis, Iron Mountain & Southern Ry. Co.* v *Craft*, 237 U. S. 648 (June 1, 1915); Aff. 171 S. W. 1185. Approved in *Kansas City S. Ry.* v *Leslie*, 238 U. S. 599.

Conscious pain and suffering, endured by employe before his death, as well as pecuniary loss to next of kin, are elements for which damages are recoverable.

> *St. Louis &c Ry.* v *Craft*, 237 U. S. 648; 35 S. C. 704; Aff. 171 S. W. 1185.
>
> *Kansas City S. Ry.* v *Leslie*, 238 U. S. 599; 35 S. C. 844; 59 L. Ed. —; Rev. 112 Ark. 305; 167 S. W. 83.
>
> *St. Louis &c Ry.* v *Conarty*, 155 S. W. 93.

Where death is instantaneous, pecuniary loss alone may be considered.

> *Norfolk &c Ry.* v *Holbrook*, 235 U. S. 625.

Action for Death—Damages—Apportionment of—

"This Act is substantially like Lord Campbell's Act, except that it omits the requirement that the jury should apportion the damages. That omission clearly indicates an intention on the part of Congress to change what was the English practice so as to make the Federal statute conform to what was the rule in most of the States in which it was to operate. Those statutes, when silent on the subject, have generally been construed not to require juries to make an apportionment."

Central Vt. Ry. Co. v *White,* 238 U. S. 508.

Damages for pain and pecuniary loss need not be separately specified in verdict.

"The language of the statute does not expressly require the jury to report what was assessed by them on account of each distinct liability, and in view of the prevailing contrary practice in similar proceedings we cannot say that a provision to that effect is necessarily implied."

Kansas City Southern Ry. v *Leslie,* 238 U. S. 599; Rev. 112 Ark. 305 (1915).

Verdict need not apportion damages for pain and suffering and those for pecuniary loss.

St. Louis &c Ry. v *Rodgers,* 176 S. W. 696.

St. Louis &c Ry. v *Craft,* 237 U. S. 648; 35 S. Ct. 704.

Verdict failing to specify amount for decedent's suffering and that for pecuniary loss, is not reversible error, when in accord with local practice.

Kansas City &c Ry. v *Leslie,* 238 U. S. 599; 35 S. Ct. 844; Rev. 112 Ark. 305; 167 S. W. 83.

Verdict should show sum allowed each beneficiary.

Hardwicks v *Wabash R. R.,* 181 Mo. App. 156; 168 S. W. 328.

A general verdict may be returned for plaintiff for benefit of widow and minor children, without apportionment to each.

Central Vermont Ry. v *White,* 238 U. S. 508; S. Ct. 865; Aff. 87 Vt. 330; 89 A. 616.

Verdict should apportion amounts according to individual loss of each beneficiary.

Collins v *Penna. R. R.,* 148 N. Y. S. 777; 163 App. Div. 452.

Action for Death—Allegations necessary—

"The existence of a beneficiary within the description of the statute, is a necessary prerequisite—an issuable fact—and therefore must be alleged and proved."

> *Melzner* v *Northern Pac. Ry.*, 46 Mont. 277 ; 127 Pac. 1002.

Complaint failing to allege that decedent left wife or child, defective.

> *Farley* v *New York &c Ry.*, 87 Conn. 328 : 87 A. 990.

Count for benefit of mother must allege that decedent left no widow or children.

> *Moffett* v *Baltimore &c Ry.*, 220 Fed. 39 ; 135 C. C. A. 607.

Complaint must allege that beneficiaries named are alive and name survivors.

> *Illinois Central Ry.* v *Porter*, 207 F. 311 ; 125 C. C. A. 55.

Declaration alleging that suit was brought for benefit of "widow and next of kin," not fatally defective for not alleging for benefit of "surviving widow and children."

> *Hale* v *Vandalia R. R.*, 169 Ill. App. 12.

Capacity to sue must be shown.

> *Martin* v *Butte Ry.*, 34 Mont. 281 ; 86 Pac. 264.

Pecuniary Loss:

"The plaintiff's declaration contains no positive averment of pecuniary loss to the parents for whose benefit the suit was instituted. Nor does it set out facts and circumstances adequate to apprise the defendant with reasonable particularity that such loss in fact was suffered. Common experience teaches that financial damage to a parent by no means follows as a necessary consequence upon the death of an adult son. The plaintiff expressly declined in both courts below so to amend his declaration as to allege pecuniary loss to the parents and judgment properly went against him. We do not think remanding the case upon such amendment now would be proper."

> *Garrett* v *Louisville & N. R. R.,* 235 U. S. 308.

Pecuniary loss must be averred.

> *McCullough* v *Chicago &c Ry.,* 142 N. W. Rep. 67.

Actual deprivation of pecuniary benefit must be alleged.

> *Illinois Central Ry.* v *Doherty,* 153 Ky. 363; 155 S. W. 1119.

Declaration failing to show facts, apprising defendant of actual pecuniary loss suffered, fatally defective.

> *Garrett* v *Louisville &c Ry.,* 235 U. S. 308; 35 S. Ct. 32; Aff. 117 C. C. A. 109; 197 F. 715.

Counts to recover damages for suffering of decedent and for pecuniary loss, seek to enforce distinct liabilities.

> *Louisville &c Ry.* v *Fleming,* 69 So. Rep. 125.

FORMS
I.
Declaration for death of switchman for benefit of widow.

State of ——————

County of ——————

      In the —————— Court of —————— County.

    1. ——————, plaintiff, Administrator of the estate of ——————, deceased, duly appointed by the —————— Court of —————— County, in the State of ——————, as such Administrator, and as the personal representative of —————— and ——————, the surviving widow and only surviving child of said deceased, by ——————, his attorney, complains of ——————, a corporation, defendant, in a plea of trespass on the case, under the Statute enacted by Congress on the 22nd day of April, 1908, entitled "An Act relating to the liability of common carriers by rail to their employes in certain cases," and the Act of Amendment thereof of the 5th day of April, 1910, and alleges:

    2. That, in the lifetime of plaintiff's said intestate, prior to and on to-wit, the —— day of ——————, the said defendant owned, possessed and operated a certain railroad extending, among other places from the City of —————— in the County of —————— in the State of ——————, into and through a part of another state, to-wit, ——————, and other states, and it was then and there a common carrier by railroad and as such was then and there engaged upon, by and in connection with its said railroad, in commerce as a carrier of passengers and freight between the several states.

    3. That said ——————, deceased, was then and there and at the time of his injuries and death, hereinafter complained of, employed by said defendant, as such common carrier by rail, engaged in commerce between the several states, as a switchman to work and switch with a

certain engine and certain cars which said defendant was then operating upon its said railroad in its said business.

4. That on, to-wit, the said —— day of ——————, at, to-wit, in the vicinity of ————th and ————th streets, in the City of ——————, in the County and State aforesaid, defendant was operating its certain switching train aforesaid, being drawn by its said locomotive upon and along one of the tracks of its said sailroad; and the said deceased, in the discharge of his duty as such switchman, was then and there standing on top of one of the cars of said train, and while the deceased was so standing upon said car, and while he was exercising ordinary care and caution for his own safety, the defendant's engineer, who was then and there in charge of the operation and management of said engine, then and there wrongfully and negligently caused said train to be stopped with great and unusual suddenness, force and violence; and as a direct result, and in consequence of said manner in which said train was so stopped, the deceased was thereby then and there and thereby thrown from said car of said train, upon which he was riding as aforesaid, to and upon the track there, and he thereby then and there sustained such serious bodily injuries that he died as a result thereof within a short time, to-wit, within an hour after said accident, in the county and state aforesaid, during which period he suffered intense and excruciating pain, suffering and agony; that said injuries occurred while said deceased was performing his duties in the employment of said defendant as aforesaid in connection with its said business as a common carrier by railroad between the several states.

5. That the deceased, said plaintiff's intestate, left him surviving his widow, ——————, and his only child, a minor son, ——————, who are still living; that the said deceased, at the time of his death was of the age of

———— years and that his earning capacity was ————
dollars per month; that said deceased was the sole support of his said surviving widow and son and regularly
contributed for their entire support; that said deceased
would probably have contributed during his life expectancy the sum of ———— dollars per month for their support; and that by reason of the foregoing the said widow
and minor son of said deceased have been deprived of the
protection, advice and aid of said deceased, and otherwise suffered great pecuniary loss.

6.   To the damage of the plaintiff as such administrator and the personal representative of said widow and
minor son of said deceased and for their benefit, and on
behalf of said decedent, for his cause of action herein, in
the sum of ———— dollars.

———————————————

Attorney for Plaintiff.
(See *Devine* v *Chicago &c Ry.,* 185 Ill. App. 488.)

Allegation for death from defective track for sister.

That heretofore, to-wit, on the —— day of ————,
in the County of ———— and State of ————,
plaintiff's intestate was a locomotive fireman in the em-
ploy of the defendant and was performing his duties as
such on a certain passenger train, engaged by said
defendant as a common carrier in interstate commerce, and · running from the City of ———— in
the State of ————, to the City of ———— in the
State of ————; that it was the duty of the defendant to exercise reasonable care to provide a reasonably
safe track on which to operate said train; that in disre-
gard of said duty the defendant negligently furnished
and maintained a defective track with insufficient rail
and rails not properly spiked to the ties, and decayed
and rotten ties, which defects defendant knew or in the
exercise of reasonable care would have known; that by
reason of said defects the locomotive of defendant's said
moving train was then and there thrown from the said
track, and the plaintiff's intestate was thereby and as a
direct result of said defects and said negligence, and
while he was in the exercise of reasonable care and while
in the performance of his duties as aforesaid, with great
force and violence, thrown upon the ground and among
the debris there and instantly killed.

That said deceased was a single man, —— years of
age, with an earning capacity and average earnings of
———— dollars per month; that he left him surviving no
widow or children, nor any parent, but a sister, named
————, who is his sister and still living and his only
surviving next of kin; that the deceased was in the habit
of contributing to the support and for the pecuniary assistance of his said sister the sum of ———— dollars
per month, and that he probably would have contributed
or given to his said sister the total sum of ———— dollars, in which amount the said ———— has suffered
pecuniary loss by the premises aforesaid, etc.

(See *Lee v Toledo &c Ry.*, 190 Ill. App. 383.)

Allegation for Excessive Speed

Plaintiff further avers that on, to-wit, the —— day of ————, in the County of ———— and State of ————, defendant was engaged as such common carrier by railroad in commerce between the several states, and plaintiff was then and there employed by defendant in such interstate commerce and engaged therein as a ————; that in the performance of his said duties it was plaintiff's duty to get upon the front end of a certain train, then and there operated by said defendant in such interstate commerce when it reached him, and it was then and there the duty of defendant's engineer thereon to run at so slow speed that plaintiff might get safely upon the same; that the said engineer then and there violated his said duty and negligently ran at a high and dangerous rate of speed and not at a moderate and safe speed, as he should have done, which defendant, through its said servant, the said engineer, then knew, and plaintiff did not know; and that while plaintiff in the exercise of due care and caution for his own safety was attempting to get on said train, he was by reason of defendant's aforesaid negligence, suddenly jerked and thrown under the train and upon the ground there and his right lower limb was severed from his body and he suffered great pain and agony, etc.

See

Mattocks v *Chicago &c Ry.*, 187 Ill. App. 529.
St. Louis v *Hesterly* (Ark.) 135 S. W. 874.

Declaration for Violation of Safety Appliance Act.

STATE OF ——————
COUNTY OF ——————
IN THE —————— COURT OF —————— COUNTY
——————, plaintiff, by ——————, his attorney, complains of ——————, a corporation, defendant, of a plea of trespass on the case.

In that whereas, plaintiff alleges, that prior to and on, to wit, ——————, the defendant owned, possessed and operated a certain railroad in the county and state aforesaid and it was then and there a common carrier by railroad and as such was then and there engaged upon, by and in connection with its said railroad, in interstate commerce and traffic;

And plaintiff was then and there and at the time of the injuries hereinafter complained of, employed by the defendant in such commerce on said interstate highway railroad as a switchman to work and switch with certain of defendant's engines and cars, which defendant was then and there operating upon its said railroad in such interstate commerce, and as such switchman earning, to wit, —————— dollars per month;

And the plaintiff further alleges that at the time and place aforesaid, to wit, at the defendant's railway yards at or near, to wit, —————— Streets, in the City of —————— in the county and state aforesaid, and which yards it operated in connection with and as part of its said railroad and its said business as a common carrier by railroad for interstate traffic, the defendant unlawfully and negligently, and contrary to the certain Acts of Congress in such case made and provided, hauled and permitted to be hauled and used upon its said railroad in moving such interstate traffic, a certain car equipped with a certain coupler, which coupler by reason of its defective and inoperative condition was not constructed nor maintained according to the provisions and requirements of the Acts of Congress in such case made and provided in that ——————;

And the plaintiff further alleges that he, as such switchman, was then and there required by the defendant in the performance of his duties as aforesaid in connection with the said business of said defendant of operating a railroad for interstate commerce traffic, to and did * * and that while in the discharge of his said duties on said car, which was then and there being moved en route from the City of ——————— in the county and state aforesaid, to the City of ————, in the State of ——————, and while he was in all respects exercising ordinary care for his own safety, he was, as a direct result and in consequence of said defective, inoperative and unlawful condition of said coupler, and in consequence of his being so required to ————— and the performance thereof, caught by his right arm between said cars and the same was crushed between the said couplers, and divers of the bones, ligaments, muscles, tendons and membranes of his said arm were thereby then and there sprained, dislocated, broken and otherwise injured, and plaintiff was cut, bruised and wounded in his head, face, limbs and body, and he sustained serious injuries to divers of his internal organs and serious shocks and injuries to his spine, nervous system and brain; and plaintiff alleges that as a result of his said injuries he has ever since suffered and will continue permanently to suffer great pain, and his said arm has become and is permanently disfigured and crippled, and its use has become and is greatly and permanently impaired, and that as a direct result of his said injuries plaintiff has become and is permanently incapacitated from attending to and transacting his regular work and business or any ordinary work, or business or affairs, and he has thereby been and will continue permanently to be deprived of large earnings, which he might and otherwise would have made and acquired, and he has been compelled to and did incur expenses and lay out, and will continue to be required to incur expenses and lay out for medical attention, nursing, medicines and otherwise, divers large amounts of money, amounting to, to wit, the sum of ——————— dollars in and about endeavoring to be cured of his said injuries, sickness and disorders occasioned as aforesaid.

To the damage of the plaintiff in the sum of —————— dollars, wherefore he brings his suit.

————————————

Attorney for Plaintiff.

Allegations for Death of Yard Clerk.

That on, to wit, ————— in the County of —————
and State of —————, the defendant owned and operated
a double track steam railroad, extending through the
said State of ————— into the State of ————— and
other states, and running through the City of —————,
in said County, wherein it maintained and operated in
connection with its said railroad many side tracks and
switches in what was called its yards;

That plaintiff's decedent was then and there employed by the defendant in the capacity of yard master and
yard clerk, and that his duties, among other things, required him to direct the setting and movement of freight
cars and to keep a record of cars shipped to and from the
said City of —————; that in the performance of his
said duties decedent was required by said defendant daily
to visit the said yards and be upon and near the tracks
aforesaid and personally inspect the cars thereon and
make a record thereof; that while engaged in such yards
at the time and place aforesaid, to wit, at or near the in-
tersection of ————— Streets in said City of —————,
and while so performing his duties as he was required by
his said employment to do in taking the numbers of certain
cars and making records thereof, which cars had then and
there arrived in said City of ————— in said State, from
the City of ————— in the State of —————, and which
were then and there loaded with interstate freight, and
while decedent was using ordinary care for his own safety, the said defendant did then and there, by its certain
locomotive engineer, negligently and wrongfully drive
and permit to be driven a certain engine, with its tender
in front, over the track whereon decedent was standing,
as it was his duty to do, on one of said defendant's tracks,
at an unusual, excessive and dangerous rate of speed, to
wit, at the rate of ————— miles an hour, and as a direct
result and in consequence of said negligence of said de-

fendant and its said engineer, decedent was then and thereby run over and killed instantaneously.

And plaintiff alleges that the said engineer could by keeping a lookout, as it was his duty to do, have perceived that said decedent was then and there standing upon said track and by using care, as it was his duty to do, avoid said accident, and that said engineer negligently, just before driving said engine over said decedent, failed to sound the whistle or ring the bell of said engine or give to decedent any warning of said approach, as it was his duty to do, and plaintiff further alleges that said engineer negligently failed to watch said track and use due care to avoid injury to plaintiff, whereby said engineer could have perceived decedent and been able to stop said engine in time to avoid said injury, etc.

See *Pittsburgh &c Ry. Co.* v *Farmers &c Trust Co.*, 108 N. E. 108.

General and Special Demurrer.

STATE OF —————

COUNTY OF —————

IN THE ————— COURT

————— Plaintiff Case.

vs. General Number —————

————— Defendant Term number —————

And the defendant, ————— by —————, its attorney comes and defends the wrong and injury when etc., and says that the declaration of the plaintiff and each and every count thereof and charge therein and the matters therein contained, are not sufficient in law for the plaintiff to have or maintain his aforesaid action against it. the said defendant, and that the defendant is not bound by law to answer the same, and this the defendant is ready to verify.

And the defendant states and shows to the Court the following causes of special demurrer to the said declaration and each count thereof, that is to say: etc.

—————————————

Attorney for Defendant.

Plea of General Issue.

And now comes the defendant, —————, by —————, its attorney, and denies the wrong and injury when etc., and says that it is not guilty of the said grievances in the manner and form as plaintiff has above thereof complained against it in his said declaration and each and all counts thereof and of this it puts itself upon the country.

—————————————

Attorney for Defendant.

SAFETY ACTS

(In relation to the Federal Employers' Liability Act)

(Act March 2, 1893, c. 196, § 1. 27 Stat. 531. Comp. Stat. vol. 4, § 8605.) **Driving wheel brakes and appliances for train-brake system.**

From and after the first day of January, eighteen hundred and ninety-eight, it shall be unlawful for any common carrier engaged in interstate commerce by railroad to use on its line any locomotive engine in moving interstate traffic not equipped with a power driving wheel brake and appliances for operating the train-brake system, or to run any train in such traffic after said date that has not a sufficient number of cars in it so equipped with power or train brakes that the engineer on the locomotive drawing such train can control its speed without requiring brakemen to use the common hand brake for that purpose.

(Act 1893, c. 196, § 2.) **Automatic couplers.**

On and after the first day of January, eighteen hundred and ninety-eight it shall be unlawful for any such common carrier to haul or permit to be hauled or used on its line any car used in moving interstate traffic not equipped with couplers coupling automatically by impact and which can be uncoupled without the necessity of men going between the end of the cars. (27 Stat. 531.)

(Act 1893, c. 196, § 3.) **Cars not so equipped may be refused by roads.**

When any person, firm, company or corporation engaged in interstate commerce by railroad shall have equipped a sufficient number of its cars so as to comply with the provisions of Section one of this act, it may lawfully refuse to receive from connecting lines of road or shippers any cars not equipped sufficiently in accordance with the first section of this Act, with such power or train brakes as will work and readily interchange with the brakes in use on its own cars, as required by this Act. (27 Stat. 531.)

(Act 1893, c. 196, § 4.) **Grab irons.**

From and after the first day of July, eighteen hundred and ninety-five, until otherwise ordered by the interstate commerce commission, it shall be unlawful for any railroad company to use any car in interstate commerce that is not provided with secure grab irons or handholds in the ends and sides of each car for greater security to men in coupling and uncoupling cars. (27 Stat. 531.)

(Act 1893, c. 196, § 5.) **Determination of standard height of drawbars for freight cars.**

Notice of standard by interstate commerce commission. Cars not complying prohibited. Logging cars excepted.   *   *   *   (27 Stat. 532; 29 Stat. 85.)

(Act 1893, c. 196, § 7.) **Commission may extend time for compliance with Act.**   *   *   *   (27 Stat. 532.)

(Act 1893, c. 196, § 8.) **Employe injured not assuming risk from violation of Act.**

Any employe of any such common carrier who may be injured by any locomotive, car, or train in use contrary to the provisions of this Act, shall not be deemed thereby to have assumed the risk thereby occasioned (although continuing in the employment of such carrier after the unlawful use of such locomotive, car or train had been brought to his knowledge. (27 Stat. 532.)

(Act March 2, 1903, c. 976, § 1.) **Provisions of Act requiring automatic couplers, continuous brakes, driving wheel brakes, grab irons and height of drawbars extended.** * * * (32 Stat. 943.)

(Act 1903, c. 976, § 2.) **Fifty percentum of cars minimum to be operated by train engineer's brakes. Interstate commerce commission to fix requirements.** . . * . . * . . * * (32 Stat. 943.)

(Act April 14, 1910, c. 160, § 2.) **Hand brakes, sill steps, etc.**

On and after July first, 1911, it shall be unlawful for any common carrier subject to the provisions of this Act, to haul or permit to be hauled or used on its line any car subject to the provisions of this Act, not equipped with appliances provided for in this Act, to wit: All cars must be equipped with secure sill steps and efficient hand brakes; all cars requiring secure ladders and secure running boards shall be equipped with such ladders and running boards, and all cars having ladders shall also be equipped with secure handholds, or grab irons, on their roofs at the tops of such ladders: Provided, that in the loading and hauling of long commodities, requiring more than one car, the hand brakes may be omitted on all save one of the cars while they are thus combined for such purpose. (36 Stat. 298.)

(Act April 14, 1910, c. 160, § 4.) **Penalty and liability for defective equipment; hauling for repairs, injury to employes.**

Any common carrier subject to this Act using, hauling or permitting to be used or hauled on its line any car subject to the requirements of this Act not equipped as provided in this Act, shall be liable to a penalty of one hundred dollars for each and every such violation to be recovered as provided in Section Six of the Act of March 2, 1893, as amended April 1, 1896. Provided, that where any car shall have been properly equipped as provided in this Act and the other Acts mentioned herein, and such equipment shall have become defective or insecure while such car was being used by such carrier upon its line of railroad, such car may be hauled from the place where such equipment was first discovered to be defective or insecure, to the nearest available point where such car can be repaired, without liability for the penalties imposed by Section 4 of this Act or Section 6 of the Act of March 2, 1893, as amended by the Act of April 1, 1896, if such movement is necessary to make such repairs and such repairs cannot be made except at such repair point; and such movement or hauling of such car shall be at the sole risk of the carrier, and nothing in this section shall be construed to relieve such carrier from liability in any remedial action for the death or injury of any railroad employe caused to such employe by reason of or in connection with the movement or hauling of such car with equipment which is defective or insecure or which is not maintained in accordance with the requirements of this Act and the other Acts herein referred to; and nothing in this proviso shall be construed to permit the hauling of defective cars by means of chains instead of drawbars, in revenue trains or in association with other cars that are commercially used, unless such defective cars contain live stock or "perishable" freight. (36 Stat. 299.)

(Act May 30, 1908, c. 225, § 1.) **Safety ash pan.**

On and after the 1st day of January, 1910, it shall be unlawful for any common carrier engaged in interstate or foreign commerce by railroad to use any locomotive in moving interstate or foreign traffic not equipped with an ash pan, which can be dumped or emptied and cleaned without the necessity of any employe going under such locomotive. (35 Stat. 476.)

(Act Feb. 17, 1911, c. 103, § 1.) **"Common carriers,"** **"railroads," and "employes" defined.**

The provisions of this Act shall apply to any common carrier or carriers, their officers, agents and employes, engaged in the transportation of passengers or property by railroad in the District of Columbia, or in any Territory of the United States, or from one state or Territory of the United States or the District of Columbia to any other state or Territory of the United States or the District of Columbia, or from any place in the United States to an adjacent foreign country, or from any place in the United States through a foreign country to any other place in the United States. The term "railroad" as used in this Act shall include all the roads in use by any common carrier operating a railroad, whether owned or operated under a contract, agreement, or lease, and the term "employes" as used in this Act shall be held to mean persons actually engaged in or connected with the movement of any train. (36 Stat. 913.)

(Act February 17, 1911, c. 103, § 2.) **Safe locomotive boiler and appurtenances.**

From and after the 1st day of July, 1911, it shall be unlawful for any common carrier, its officers, or agents, subject to this Act, to use any locomotive engine propelled by steam power in moving interstate or foreign traffic unless the boiler of said locomotive and appurtenances thereof are in proper condition and safe to operate in the service to which the same is put, that the same may be employed in the active service of such carrier in moving traffic without necessary peril to life or limb, and all boilers shall be inspected from time to time in accordance with the provisions of this Act and be able to withstand such test or tests as may be prescribed in the rules and regulations hereinafter provided for. (36 Stat. 913.)

"An Act *to promote the safety of employes and travelers upon railroads by limiting the hours of service of employes thereon.*"

(Act March 4, 1907, c. 2939, § 2) **Hours of service limited.**

It shall be unlawful for any common carrier, its officers or agents, subject to this Act, to require or permit any employe subject to this Act to be or remain on duty for a longer period than sixteen consecutive hours, and wherever any such employe of such common carrier shall have been continuously on duty for sixteen hours he shall be relieved and not be required or permitted again to go on duty until he has had at least ten consecutive hours off duty; and no such employe who has been on duty sixteen hours in the aggregate in any twenty-four-hour period shall be required or permitted to continue or again go on duty without having had at least eight consecutive hours off duty. Provided, that no operator, train dispatcher, or other employe who, by the use of telegraph or telephone dispatches, reports, transmits, receives, or delivers orders pertaining to or affecting train movements shall be required or permitted to be or remain on duty for a longer period than nine hours in any twenty-four hour period in all towns, offices, places and stations continuously operated night and day, nor for a longer period than thirteen hours in all towns, offices, places and stations operated only during the day-time, except in case of emergency, when the employes named in this proviso may be permitted to be and remain on duty for four additional hours in a twenty-four hour period or not exceeding three days in any week: Provided further, the Interstate Commerce Commission may, after a full hearing in a particular case and for good cause shown extend the period within which a common carrier shall comply with the provisions of this proviso as to such case. (Act provides penalties for violation and excepts cases of unavoidable accident, where delay could not have been foreseen, wrecking crews and relief trains.) (34 Stat. 1416-1417.)

INDEX

A.

B.

INDEX

INDEX

R.

S.

INDEX

T.

ImTheStory.com

Personalized Classic Books in many genre's

Unique gift for kids, partners, friends, colleagues

Customize:

- Character Names

- Upload your own front/back cover images (optional)

- Inscribe a personal message/dedication on the

    inside page (optional)

Customize many titles Including
- Alice in Wonderland
- Romeo and Juliet
- The Wizard of Oz
- A Christmas Carol
- Dracula
- Dr. Jekyll & Mr. Hyde
- And more...

Emily's Adventures In Wonderland

Ryan & Julia

CPSIA information can be obtained at www.ICGtesting.com
Printed in the USA
LVOW10s2323200913

353479LV00029B/1282/P